# Garment Technology
## for
# Fashion Designers

Gerry Cooklin

*b*

**Blackwell
Science**

© 1997 by
Blackwell Science Ltd
Editorial Offices:
Osney Mead, Oxford OX2 0EL

Kurfürstendamm 57
10707 Berlin, Germany

Blackwell Science KK
MG Kodenmacho Building
7–10 Kodenmacho Nihombashi
Chuo-ku, Tokyo 104, Japan

First published 1997

Set in 11/12 Sabon
by DP Photosetting, Aylesbury, Bucks
Printed and bound in Great Britain by
Hartnolls Ltd, Bodmin, Cornwall

The Blackwell Science logo is a
trade mark of Blackwell Science Ltd,
registered at the United Kingdom
Trade Marks Registry

DISTRIBUTORS

Marston Book Services Ltd
PO Box 269
Abingdon
Oxon OX14 4YN
(*Orders:* Tel: 01235 465500
            Fax: 01235 465555)

USA
  Blackwell Science, Inc.
  Commerce Place
  350 Main Street
  Malden, MA 02148 5018
  (*Orders:* Tel: 800 759 6102
                  617 388 8250
             Fax: 617 388 8255)

Canada
  Copp Clark Professional
  200 Adelaide Street West, 3rd Floor
  Toronto, Ontario M5H 1W7
  (*Orders:* Tel: 416 597-1616
                  800 815 9417
             Fax: 416 597 1617)

Australia
  Blackwell Science Pty Ltd
  54 University Street
  Carlton, Victoria 3053
  (*Orders:* Tel: 03 9347 0300
             Fax: 03 9347 5001)

A catalogue record for this title
is available from the British Library

ISBN 0-632-04775-5

Library of Congress
Cataloging-in-Publication Data

Cooklin, Gerry.
    Garment technology for fashion designers/
  Gerry Cooklin.
      p.    cm.
    Includes bibliographical references and
  index.
    ISBN 0-632-04775-5 (pb)
    1. Clothing trade.   2. Tailoring—Pattern
  design.   3. Garment cutting.   I. Title.
  TT497.C66   1997
  687'.04—dc21                       97-34199
                                         CIP

# Contents

# *Preface*

For more than twenty years, I have been teaching design students at Shenkar College in Ramat Gan, Israel, and have always tried to duplicate in the classroom, and through projects, the actual conditions of the working situation. In the main, this has meant helping and encouraging the students to develop a practical and comprehensive perspective on the host of activities associated with the day to day work of a fashion designer. Three of the central subjects covered in this approach are direct materials and labour costs, garment technology and the operation of the design department.

Not every clothing factory has the luxury of resident clothing technologists, which means that the designer has to make most of the technological decisions at the sampling stage. In addition, the designer has to be familiar with the production methods and constraints of the factory where the garments will be produced. Attractive samples are unsaleable if they do not slot into the targeted price bracket. This is yet another important aspect of the designer's work.

This book attempts to provide students and designers with the means to make informed decisions regarding the subjects directly related to the total objectives of garment design.

*Gerry Cooklin*

# *Acknowledgements*

My thanks are extended to the machinery manufacturers, their agents and other organisations who provided me with technical material and permission to reproduce illustrations of their products and exhibits.

| | |
|---|---|
| Ruth Bean | England |
| Investronica | Spain |
| Kannegiesser | Germany |
| Kuris | Germany |
| Maier-Unitas | Germany |
| Pfaff | Germany |
| Eike Randebrock | Germany |
| Rimoldi | Italy |
| Science Museum – | |
| Science & Society Picture Library | England |
| Veit | Germany |
| Thomas Walker | England |

## AGENTS

| | |
|---|---|
| Neel Agencies | Tel-Aviv |
| Ormi | Tel-Aviv |
| Schlein Bros. | Tel-Aviv |
| Stacy Enterprises | Raanana |
| Technotex | Tel-Aviv |

# *Introduction*

Garment design does not exist in a vacuum but is the end product of a chain of activities which can be said to start with the production of textile fibres. Various authorities have estimated that the time span between fibre production and the sampling stage is between six to eight months. For the clothing manufacturer, the internal chain of activities starts some time before the forthcoming season's materials are available because the company has to have some firmed-up ideas of what it intends doing before selecting materials.

The internal chain usually starts with the marketing department doing some formal or informal market research to evaluate what the market sector served by the company could be looking for and at what prices. Parallel to this, the designer has probably visited overseas couture houses to obtain indications of the possible trends for the next season. Marketing and design put their heads together and start formulating the framework of the sample collection. Fabrics and trimmings are selected and ordered and the designer starts to prepare the core designs which will represent the central theme garments of the collection. Core designs, when approved, will be the basis for developing planned groups of variations. The pre-sales design room processes are shown in Fig. I1.

In this context, garment design becomes goal directed planning because apart from developing the appeal factors of each design, the designer also has to take into account the many technical and commercial factors involved. So when designs have been approved and materials delivered, the design team has to start becoming very involved with the production of sample garments. This is the point at which this book starts, with the text directed at both designers and pattern cutters because in smaller factories they are likely to be the same person.

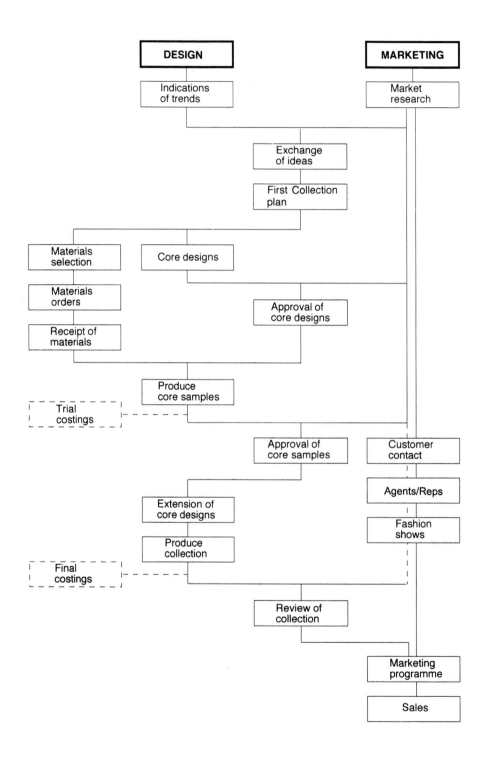

**Fig. I1.** Pre-sales design room processes.

# PART 1
## COST CONSCIOUSNESS

# 1
# *The Designer and Garment Costs*

Under a free enterprise system it is accepted by the business world that money is the name of the game, and the clothing industry is no exception. The success of designs produced by a manufacturer can only be judged by the colour printed on the company's bank statement at the end of a season: red or black. There are many factors which can influence profitability, but in normal circumstances profitability originates to a large extent in the design section.

## THE FRAMEWORK

Where does it all start for the designer? The answer is a combination of two factors:

- Market specialisation
- The average garment concept.

This linking provides the designer with a reasonably accurate basis for initial cost estimates

### MARKET SPECIALISATION

The clothing industry is divided into sectors according to garment types, and within each sector there are subdivisions or sections based primarily on price. For example, one sector could be men's dress trousers, with the sections having prices ranging from very cheap to highly expensive. The prices obviously reflect the total quality and fashion content of the products.

The majority of clothing manufacturers concentrate on serving and expanding their share of a specific section within a sector. As a result, they accumulate a great deal of expertise regarding the suitability of products, prices and production demands. Knowing this, the company is able to break down its average ex-factory price into the main components, such as materials, labour, overheads and profit. The results of this analysis provide the designer with an accurate indication of what can be invested in an average garment in terms of materials and labour. The proportions between these two cost factors can vary from style to style, but their total has to be on, or very close to, the target in order that a new sample will be able to slot into the correct price bracket.

## THE AVERAGE GARMENT CONCEPT

Most production units, irrespective of the production system employed, are built around the average garment concept where this term refers to a typical garment produced by the unit. This typical garment has an acceptable work content and the balance between the various groups of operations is reflected in the staffing and equipment of the unit. This type of factory would have the capability to handle a reasonable range of cloth and/or styling variations without serious modifications regarding staff, machinery and layout.

The average garment concept is very widely used because of the production commonalities which exist between garments of the same type. In practice this means that regardless of individual styling, nearly every garment produced goes through the same standard operations. For example, the common operations for a unit producing skirts could be: overlocking, dart-sewing, closing side seams, zip setting, preparing and setting waistbands, top and underpressing operations, finishing and inspection procedures.

It is relatively simple for production people to supply the designer with the times for each group of operations in an average garment produced by the factory. By referring to these times and to an average garment, the designer can make fairly accurate estimates of the work content of each new design. In addition, the designer can evaluate whether the operations required will fit into the production balance of the factory.

Whilst nobody expects a fashion designer to be an expert in garment costing, designers must be aware of their influence on costs. Garments have to be evaluated for costs at the sampling stage because making samples without regard to price is often futile. So when necessary, the designer and pattern maker have to modify designs and patterns so as to bring a new sample into the correct price framework.

## THE GARMENT COSTING

Also known as the bill of materials, the garment costing details the costs of every item attributable to the production of a particular garment. The sum of these costs plus the profit margin is the selling price which the company will quote to customers. Whilst each company has its own method of preparing costings, generally the components of a costing are grouped under four headings: direct materials, direct labour, factory overhead and general overhead.

## DIRECT MATERIALS

Direct materials are all the materials and trimmings which go into the construction and finish of the garment. Typically, these materials would include cloth, lining, fusibles, buttons, zips, pads, tapes, labels, tickets, hangers and packaging materials, etc.

## DIRECT LABOUR

This covers the cost of all the labour directly involved in producing the garment and could include cutting, fusing, regular sewing, special machine operations, pressing, finishing, inspection and packing. Labour of all types and grades has a direct overhead which includes holiday pay, sick pay, fringe benefits, etc, and the statutory payments made by the employer for each employee. This is usually expressed as a percentage of salary and when this percentage is added to the employee's wage, it becomes the basis for calculating direct labour costs.

## FACTORY OVERHEAD

There are different methods of calculating the factory overhead, but most of them use a combination of the following three elements:

(1) *Indirect labour*  This covers every person in the factory who does not directly perform a production operation, such as managers, supervisors, engineers, store personnel, clerks, maintenance staff, porters, canteen staff, security and cleaners, etc.
(2) *Expenses*  Included in this element is every fixed and variable expense incurred in operating the factory, such as rent, rates, utilities, insurance, depreciation, maintenance, air conditioning and the various types of energy generation required by a clothing factory.
(3) *Indirect materials*  Also known as consumables, this element contains all the materials not directly connected to the make-up of a garment. Some of the typical items involved are office materials, spare parts, marker paper, maintenance materials, chalk and pins.

The total of these three elements is the factory overhead and because it cannot be conveniently applied to specific cost units, it is generally expressed as a percentage of the direct labour costs. For example, if the costs for a given period are:

Direct labour        £28,000 (including direct overhead)
Factory overhead  £33,600

the factory overhead is 120% of the cost of direct labour. From this, it is simple to calculate the cost of one minute's work for every production operator:

| | |
|---|---|
| Labour rate per hour | £6.00 |
| Factory overhead at 120% | £7.20 |
| Total cost | £13.20 |
| Cost per work minute | £0.22 |

Therefore the price of an operation is the rate per minute multiplied by the time allowed for the operation.

## GENERAL OVERHEAD

The general overhead comprises all the labour costs and expenses which are incurred in running the company, such as management, marketing, finance, insurance, warehousing, rent and utilities. The design department costs are usually allocated to this component.

Again, because of the practical difficulties of apportioning this component to specific cost units, it is expressed as a percentage of the total for direct labour, factory overhead and direct materials, as in this example, where all the costs are for the same period:

| | |
|---|---|
| Direct materials | £84,000 |
| Direct labour | £28,000 |
| Factory overheads at 120% | £33,600 |
| Total | £145,600 |
| General overhead | £65,520 |

Therefore, conveniently, the general overhead is 45% of all the other costs. So the framework of a garment costing would be the sum total of these four components.

An example of a garment costing is shown in Fig. 1.1; the figures are for demonstration purposes only. Whilst the method of computation, detail, terminology and format can vary from company to company, the primary objectives of the costing are always the same: how much does the garment cost to produce?

## THE DESIGNER'S ROLE

The preparation of a garment costing is usually the work of a costing

| GARMENT COSTING | | | |
|---|---|---|---|
| Style number | Comp. number | Market | Description |
| 6114 | HC 20 664 | Home ✓ Export | Straight Coat |
| Season | Phase | Size range | Factory |
| Winter | 2 | 36-42 | Wigan |

| Item | Description | Supplier | Quan. | Price | Unit cost |
|---|---|---|---|---|---|
| Cloth | 100% wool - 4608 | North Mills | 2.60 | 9.40 | 24.44 |
| Lining | Satin - 856 | Lintex | 2.40 | 3.80 | 9.12 |
| Fusible | W311 - A | Fusmat | 0.90 | 2.90 | 2.61 |
| Buttons | 1142 - Size 40 | Fladom | 6 | 0.20 | 1.20 |
| Pads | Raglan - 16 | Asleh | Pair | 0.65 | 0.65 |
| Threads | Regular | Stock | / | 0.80 | 0.80 |
| Brand label | } Gerlin - 4 | Stock | 1 | 0.16 | 0.16 |
| Size label | } | | | | |
| Care label | 100% wool / Dry Clean | Stock | 1 | 0.12 | 0.12 |
| Ticket | Gerlin - A | Stock | 1 | 0.15 | 0.15 |
| Hanger | T6 | Hangetti | 1 | 0.35 | 0.35 |
| Packing | Coat Bag - 8 | Plastpac. | 1 | 0.20 | 0.20 |

| Production | Min. | Price | Cost | Materials | 39.80 |
|---|---|---|---|---|---|
| Cutting | 6 | 0.20 | 1.20 | Production | 16.33 |
| Fusing | 2 | 0.15 | 0.30 | Gen. overhead | 22.45 |
| Sewing | 55 | 0.17 | 9.35 | Total cost: | 78.58 |
| Specials | 6 | 0.17 | 1.02 | Profit | 11.78 |
| Under pressing | 6 | 0.15 | 0.90 | Commission | 4.75 |
| Top pressing | 11 | 0.18 | 1.98 | Total: | 95.11 |
| Finishing | 4 | 0.15 | 0.66 | Selling price | 95.00 |
| Inspection | 4 | 0.17 | 0.68 | Prepared by | ⟨signature⟩ |
| Packing | 2 | 0.15 | 0.36 | Date | 18/5 |
| | | | | Approved by | ⟨signature⟩ |
| Total: | 96 | Total: | 16.33 | Date | 20/5 |

Fig. 1.1. Example of garment costing.

clerk who collates all the relevant information and calculates money values. Before the costing process starts the design room needs to check and approve the basic viability of the sample garment. Skilled marker planners can reduce materials requirements, and production engineers can accurately analyse work content, but if the sample garment is carrying excessive costs of materials and/or labour, there is very little that these people can do to make the garment an acceptable proposition. So the designer has far more responsibility than just designing garments.

# 2
# Pattern Cutting and Materials Utilisation

This chapter examines the critical influence of the garment pattern on the pivotal activities in a clothing factory. There is no doubt that pattern cutting, whether performed manually or with a CAD system, is the most important technical process in the production of clothing. Apart from effective design interpretation, the pattern cutter has a major responsibility to provide the basis for the most efficient usage of materials.

## MATERIALS UTILISATION

Over the years, various researchers have established that approximately 85% of the materials purchased are in the finished garment, with the remainder for one reason or another ending up as waste. This figure is called the materials utilisation percentage and it is a crucial cost factor in the price of a garment. Materials generally comprise about 50% of the cost price of a garment with labour representing approximately 20%. So an improvement of, say, 5% in materials utilisation is worth far more than a 5% reduction in production time. Whilst the pattern cutter cannot personally prevent excess materials usage in the cutting room, there are a number of procedures which can be employed to ensure that the garment pattern makes the minimum possible demands on materials requirements. These procedures are grouped together under the heading of pattern engineering.

## PATTERN ENGINEERING

The overall objectives of pattern engineering are to improve the utilisation factor of a garment pattern through prudent modifications which do not degrade the design integrity. A line has to be drawn between the enhancement of materials utilisation and the maintenance of the design objectives. If the sweep of a fully flared dress is reduced by four to five centimetres or the width of a skirt waistband is decreased by two or three millimetres, would these modifications make any material difference to the final appearance of the garment? If pattern modifications are planned, they should be considered with a large measure of common sense.

The central procedures of pattern engineering are pattern accuracy, major modifications and making up allowances.

## PATTERN ACCURACY

Pattern accuracy is a fundamental subject. It is said, with justification, that apart from cutting mistakes, the accuracy of a pattern cutter can be judged by the amount and size of the cuttings found on the sewing room floor. Production operators are not supposed to be cutters and if they have to remove surpluses from components because of incorrect pattern alignments or erroneous allowances, then only the pattern cutter is to blame. Apart from the wasted materials, the production operators are to some extent prevented from doing the work they are paid to do, so this situation is a two-fold loss for the company. It can be eliminated to a large extent by greater precision on the part of the pattern cutter.

## MAJOR MODIFICATIONS

These modifications could include seam displacements, slight reductions in flare, splitting very large components, separate instead of extended facings, etc. Some examples are shown in Fig. 2.1. These, and other similar major modifications, require a pragmatic type of flexibility from the designer and pattern cutter because, design considerations apart, every saving in materials is a potential advantage for the company.

It is worth remembering that whilst many of today's consumers are design and quality literate, they are still not clothing technicians, so a small element of 'bluff' is permissible.

## MAKING UP ALLOWANCES

This covers seam and hem allowances and facing widths. According to an American survey (Hudson, 1989), seam and hem allowances together account for approximately 5.5% of the material used for the actual garment. So it is up to the pattern cutter to ensure that all these allowances are the practical minimum possible.

# SEAMS

The most important properties of a seam are strength and flexibility and these are determined by a number of technical factors plus the char-

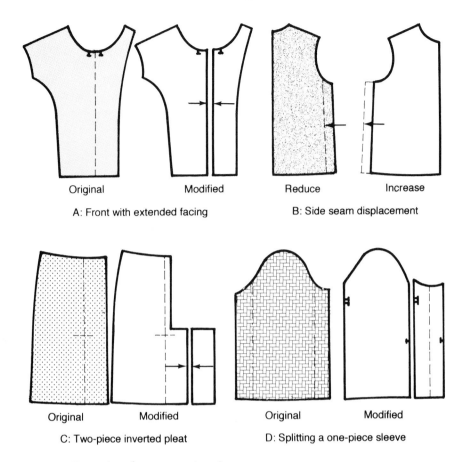

Original    Modified         Reduce       Increase

A: Front with extended facing      B: Side seam displacement

Original    Modified         Original       Modified

C: Two-piece inverted pleat       D: Splitting a one-piece sleeve

**Fig. 2.1.** Examples of pattern engineering.

acteristics of the fabric and the width of the seam allowance. Some of the more important technical factors are examined in Chapter 8, whilst a more comprehensive treatment can be found in Carr and Latham (1994), Friend (1977) and Solinger (1988).

The width of seam allowances is primarily decided by the characteristics of the fibre to be sewn and the type of seam being sewn. In order to establish an appropriate background for the examination of these two factors, the construction elements of the most commonly used seam will be analysed. This seam, referred to as a superimposed seam, is constructed by sewing two components together along one edge of each piece (Fig. 2.2), and the seam is usually pressed open.

Over many years, the clothing industry has proved that for regularly constructed fabrics, the optimal seam margin for assembly seams is 1 cm. This width combines three important elements:

(1)  *Lateral strength* (Fig. 2.3)  In this context, strength refers to the ability of the seam to withstand reasonable pressures at angles to its length.

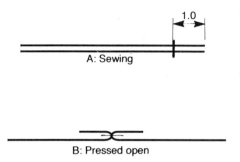

Fig. 2.2. Regular assembly seam.

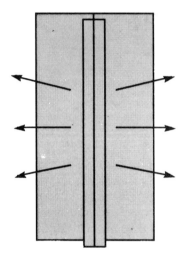

Fig. 2.3. Lateral pressure on seam.

(2) *Handling* The width is sufficient for the presser to open the seam easily by hand when pressing it open.

(3) *Visual Control* (Fig. 2.4) For operator controlled seaming there has to be an adequate margin between the right hand side of the pressure foot and the edge of the seam being sewn. When using a regular presser foot this margin enables the operator to visually control seam width.

It is generally accepted that loosely constructed materials require slightly larger seam allowances than those for more tightly woven fabrics. There are no rules governing this additional allowance, but in many cases, 2 or 3 mm would be sufficient. If in doubt, it is worth testing seam strength before making a decision, because wider seam allowances are not necessarily required for every type of loosely constructed fabric. The allowances for the main type of standard seams are given here.

## EDGES (FIG. 2.5)

These are enclosed seams which are typically used for the edges of collars, lapels and flaps, etc. For profile or jig-sewing a seam width of 5 mm is used, and for operator controlled edge sewing 6 mm. In both cases, if the sewing machine also has an edge trimming action, an additional 2 mm is necessary.

## KNITS

Garments made from knits are nearly always assembled by overlock or safety-stitch machines and the basic seam allowance is derived from the bight of the machine to be used. The bight refers to the finished seam width produced by the machine and to this an allowance of 2 or 3 mm has to be added for edge trimming.

## LAP FELLED SEAMS (FIG. 2.6)

Commonly used for jeans and similarly styled garments, the seam allowance is determined by the needle gauge of the machine to be used. The needle gauge is the measurement between the centres of the two needles and the seam allowance is calculated as follows:

1.5 (needle gauge) + 1 mm

For example, given a needle gauge of 8 mm, the seam allowance would be:

12 mm + 1 mm = 13 mm

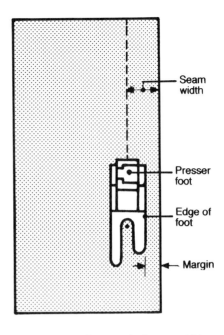

Fig. 2.4.   Visual Control of seam width.

## TOP STITCHED SEAMS

The two elements which determine the sewing allowances for these seams are the width of the top stitching and the thickness of the material. For very light weight materials, the seam margin is the width of the top stitching plus 2 or 3 mm (Fig. 2.7). If the edges of the seam are to be overlocked, an addition of 2 or 3 mm is necessary.

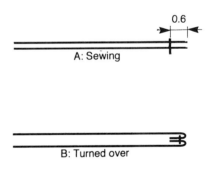

Fig. 2.5.   Enclosed seam for edges.

On heavy materials this method would produce a thick, stiff seam and this can be remedied by using different allowances on the two components which are to be joined and top-stitched. For the top component, which is top stitched, the sewing allowance is the width of the top stitch minus 3 mm. The

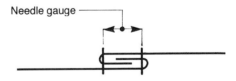

Fig. 2.6.   Lap felled seam (jeans).

allowance on the under component is the top stitch width plus 3 mm. Fig. 2.8 illustrates the application of these allowances and it can be seen that the resultant seam construction would be thinner and more pliable than if the two components had the same seam widths.

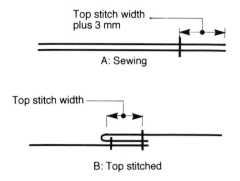

**Fig. 2.7.**   Top stitching on light weight materials.

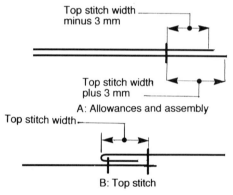

**Fig. 2.8.**   Top stitching on heavy weight materials.

## OTHER SEAM TYPES

An enormous variety of seam constructions is used in the clothing industry and it is beyond the scope of this book to examine the allowances for all of them. Some of the allowances can be pre-determined by the apparatus employed to construct the seam, whilst others are derived from the width of a material which is to be applied to, or inserted in, a seam. It is always worth checking carefully what exactly is required and, if there is any doubt, experimentation is advisable.

## FINAL WORD ON SEAM ALLOWANCES

Modern sizing technology ensures that the majority of consumers can purchase garments which do not require alterations to girths except possibly, skirt and trouser waistbands. Consequently there is no real practical reason to include allowances on the pattern for increasing the girths of body garments. Wider than necessary seam allowances are sometimes used for skirts and dresses, and these seams are supposedly an indication of garment quality. This approach is perfectly acceptable if it is company policy, as long as the company understands that these seams are an additional cost factor

## HEMS

This refers to the turn-ups on the lower extremities of body garments, skirts, trousers and sleeves etc., and the same considerations apply to both the top-cloth and lining. The guiding principle for this group of allowances is that they should be just sufficient for their purpose but no more. There is no need to allow for the possible lengthening of a garment because normal height differences are usually catered for by the standard short, medium and tall size ranges. It is impossible to provide hem allowances that will cover every possible eventuality of height variations.

A garment or sleeve hem, apart from the finish which it imparts, also gives a certain amount of weight and stability to the hem line. Both these elements have a beneficial influence on the finished appearance of a garment, thus contributing to its overall quality. Different garment types have varying requirements as regards acceptable hem widths and the general industrial practice is:

*Body garments – outerwear and light clothing*   Garment hems 4 cm. Sleeve hems 3.5–4 cm.

*Trousers and skirts – outerwear and light clothing*   Hems 3.5 cm.

*Woven blouses and shirts*   Hem width gross 1.2 cm.

Both the body and sleeve hems are usually double-turned by standard folders. and Figure 2.9 shows this hem formation and the difference between the gross and net widths. If the sleeve is not finished with an attached or extended cuff, the gross turn-up width is 2.2 cm.

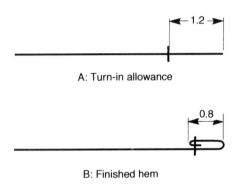

Fig. 2.9.   Double turn hem for shirts and blouses.

*Cut knits, for example, leisure shirts and blouses*   Garment hems 2.0 cm. Sleeve hems 2.0 cm.

Manufacturers of cut knits have standard single turn folders (Fig. 2.10) on their hemming machines and the pattern has to have an allowance which matches the folder plus 2 or 3 mm for edge trimming.

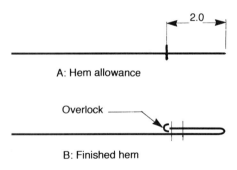

Fig. 2.10.   Single turn hem for cut knits.

### Flared hems

In all cases when the body or sleeve hem is flared, the standard hem allowance should be reduced in order to ensure a flat laying turn-in. For very flared hem lines, such as that of a circular skirt, the allowance can be as little as 8 mm plus 2–3 mm for overlocking.

## LINING HEMS

There are two types of hem allowances for linings and the type used depends on whether the lining hem is sewn to the garment or is left open.

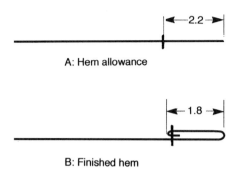

A: Hem allowance

B: Finished hem

**Fig. 2.11.** Double turn hem for open linings.

- *Sewn hems* The allowance for sewn lining hems is derived directly from the hem widths of the body and sleeve. No savings can be made, apart from not exaggerating shrinkage and ease allowances.
- *Open hems* (Fig. 2.11) These are mostly used for flared garments because the lining hem sweep is usually less than that of the garment as the lining only needs to have sufficient sweep to allow for a comfortable stride length.

## FACING WIDTHS

For practical purposes, the width of a front facing depends to a large extent on the direction of the buttonholes in relation to the front edge. There are two standard directions:

- *Vertical* Where the buttonholes are parallel to the front edge.
- *Horizontal* Where the buttonholes are at right angles to the front edge.

The factors which govern the calculation of the relevant facing widths are given here.

### Vertical buttonholes (Fig. 2.12A)
Vertical buttonholes are nearly always located on the centre front line of single breasted garments; typical examples are blouses and shirts. If the garment has an attached or extended placket down the forepart, the facing width is the same as the placket plus whatever allowances are needed for assembly and finishing. This calculation also applies to garments having an inset placket, such as polo shirts.

### Horizontal buttonholes (Fig. 2.12B)
Facings for garments with horizontal buttonholes can, for demonstration purposes, be divided into two sections:

- *Section 1* From the shoulder to the top buttonhole
- *Section 2* From the top buttonhole down to the hem

The details which have to be taken into account when calculating the width of the lower section (section 2) are:

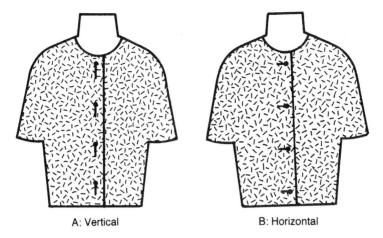

A: Vertical          B: Horizontal

**Fig. 2.12.** Buttonhole directions.

- The distance between the eye of the buttonhole and the front edge, usually equal to half the diameter of the button plus 5 or 6 mm.
- The length of the buttonhole itself, which is based on the diameter and thickness of the button.
- An allowance from the end of the buttonhole to the inside edge of the facing, which needs to be sufficient to allow for blindstitching and lining setting.

These details are illustrated in Fig. 2.13 and their total provides the width of the lower section.

If the garment is unlined and not blindstitched, apart from an allowance for overlocking, the facing should extend past the end of the buttonhole so as to enable the foot of the buttonhole machine to clamp down on to a flat surface. A total of 12–15 mm would be adequate for these two allowances.

The width and run of the facing's upper section are based on whether a label is attached to the back neck piece. It is preferable for the combined inside edge of the neck piece and facing to be a smooth, continuous line for its whole length. If a label is positioned on the neck piece, the width of the neck piece has to be sufficient to contain the label plus a small margin all round. Thus the total net width of the neck piece pro-

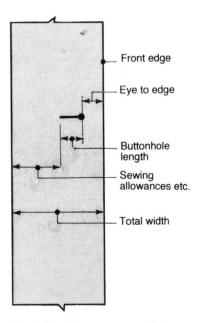

Front edge

Eye to edge

Buttonhole length

Sewing allowances etc.

Total width

**Fig. 2.13.** Components of facing width.

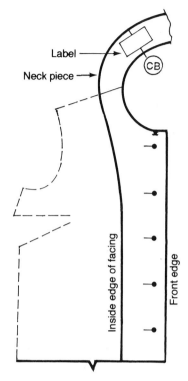

**Fig. 2.14.** Run of neck piece and facing.

vides the start of the inside edge line which runs down to the lower section (Fig. 2.14). Where the label is attached to the body lining, a net back piece width of 4 cm is sufficient for most purposes.

## CUT TRIMMINGS

Other areas of materials utilisation include trimmings which have to be cut, as against trim which is purchased ready-made. The two most widely used cut trimmings are fusibles and linings, and as together, they represent a significant cost component of garments, the patterns for these materials also have to contain only the practical minimum possible.

## FUSIBLES

Pattern cutting for fusibles is examined in Chapter 6; here we deal with the pattern engineering aspects. The effect of fusibles on the finished appearance of a garment can be seen, whereas the fusibles themselves cannot be seen. This allows for some creative pattern engineering to be applied.

### INTERLOCKING COMPONENTS

On many garments, the fusibles for some of the components are cut from the same material. This provides an excellent opportunity for the pattern cutter to maximise the potential for tightly interlocking components, which has two benefits:

- Waste is decreased because the spaces between components are reduced or completely eliminated.
- When, say, two components are completely interlocked by means of a common line, then only one line instead of two has to be cut to separate components – a small but worthwhile saving of labour.

Unlike pattern modifications to top cloth components, there is only one question to be asked regarding the form of a pattern for a fusible:

'If the fusible is not intended to completely cover the cloth component, then is the form of the edges of the fusible – which do not have to align with the edges of the component – important?'

The following examples show different applications of interlocking. The first is a demonstration of the principles involved.

### Example 1
These are two standard components which have to be cut from an omnidirectional, non-woven fusible:

(1) *Lapel facing* This covers the lapel section only and extends for 2 or 3 cm over the crease line.

(2) *Under collar* Cut to the exact shape of the cloth under collar.

Fig. 2.15A shows how these two components were originally positioned in the cutting marker, with the resultant waste plus the necessity for cutting two lines in order to separate them. After modifications to the lapel fusible, the interlocking of the two components is illustrated in Fig. 2.15B. This new pattern arrangement has resulted in a reduction of waste and one common cutting line between the two pieces.
  The line of the lapel fusible is a non-functional line and is distanced from the crease line only to ensure that the crease line is covered, with something to spare. Three changes have been made to this particular line:

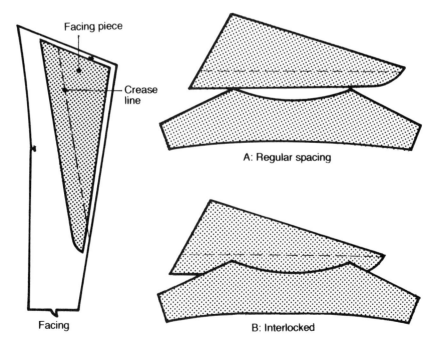

**Fig. 2.15.**  Example of interlocking – facing piece and under collar.

(1) It has a small V notch in its upper section
(2) The curve of the collar's neck seam has been incorporated into part of its width
(3) Whilst the length has been slightly reduced and the form of the end has been changed, the piece still covers the top buttonhole.

These three modifications have not made the slightest difference to the functionality of the component but have produced changes for the better as regards materials usage and cutting time. Again fusibles are not seen, so some 'doctoring' of the nonfunctional lines is permissible, especially when this operation results in savings.

### Example 2

Conventionally a partially fused front runs from the shoulder to the hem line and from a point on the armhole also to the hem line. The shoulder, armhole, neck and front edge lines are 100% functional, but the line from the armhole to the hem is non-functional. This particular line is really only a shaped line which connects a selected point on the armhole to a point on the hem line. The distance of this last point from the front edge only has to be sufficient to catch the blind-stitching of the facing, which is generally about 2 cm from the gross inside edge of the facing itself.

Fig. 2.16A shows the original positioning of a pair of these components in the cutting marker, with the ensuing waste and the need to cut

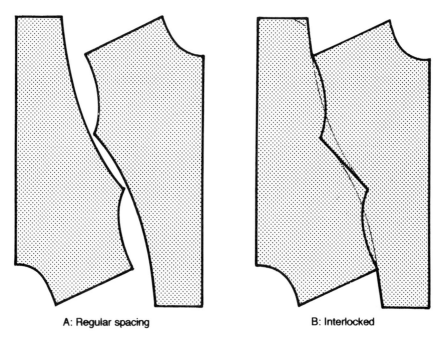

A: Regular spacing          B: Interlocked

**Fig. 2.16.** Example of interlocking – front fusibles.

two lines. Fig. 2.16B illustrates the level of interlocking which can be achieved through rational pattern modifications. A reduction in waste and the elimination of one line are both brought about by pattern changes which have no influence on functionality.

### General considerations
Where possible these pieces should be of one length and one form only for all sizes. For example, if the seam allowance on both of the cloth sleeve underseams is, say 1 cm, the fact that the hem fusible will be a little too long or a little too short on some sizes is not particularly relevant because:

- Excess length is easily disregarded by the operator who sews the underseam
- The lack of a few millimetres at this position on the sleeve is of no real consequence.

Combining one length and one shape also has the advantage that the grading of this piece is eliminated and the cutting room is not required to separate different sizes.

Patterns for fusible components have much potential for modifications which can result in worthwhile savings of materials and time. This is another important aspect of the pattern cutter's work.

## LININGS

Linings are also an important cost component and whilst the potential for pattern modifications is limited, there are some minor procedures which can enhance the utilisation of materials. A simple and convenient work-aid which can help the pattern cutter, is to mark on his or her work table the standard width of the lining used by the factory. (A narrow, coloured adhesive tape is recommended for this purpose.) By using these marks the pattern cutter is able, at an early stage, to evaluate which pattern modifications would be viable. Some of the possible modifications are given here.

### SKIRT LININGS

Conventionally, skirt lining patterns are positioned in cutting markers according to the warp grain line of the material. If folded lining is used, this pattern arrangement generally leads to a relatively high percentage of marker waste. All clothing industry professionals know that materials utilisation is higher on open materials than on folded materials, and linings are no exception.

An option which can be used on open lining, pattern length permitting, is to position the pattern component across the lining instead of down the length (Fig. 2.17). Some purists might say that lining is stronger in its length than in its width. They are correct, but linings are firmly constructed materials and the weft direction is generally strong enough to withstand the regular pressures exerted on skirt linings. If necessary the side seams can be displaced from the hip line down. Positioning components across the fabric can also be used for trousers with knee length linings, again subject to pattern length.

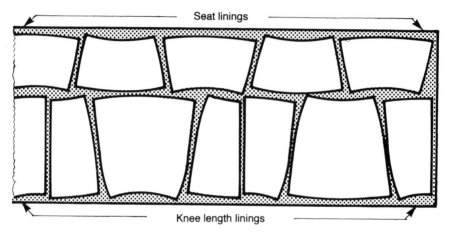

**Fig. 2.17.** An option: cutting skirt linings across the piece.

## BODY LININGS

Unlike fusibles, body linings are seen and whilst this severely limits the possibilities of major pattern modifications, there are always opportunities for improving materials utilisation. The two main components of a full lining are the body and the sleeve and the following examines what can be applied to both of them.

### The body
If the body lining patterns for a straight garment are being used to plan a cutting marker, there is always the possibility that displacing the side seams could lead to a more efficient marker. This particular displacement could take three different forms where a reasonable seam displacement of, say, 3 cm at each point is not exceeded

(1)  From zero at the armhole to a maximum of 3 cm at the hem
(2)  From zero at the hem to a maximum of 3 cm at the armhole
(3)  Displacing the entire length of the side seam up to 3 cm in either direction.

If the lining seam has been displaced at the armhole (Fig. 2.18), then the lower section of armhole on the extended component should be nipped in order to indicate to the operator who tacks this area of the lining that the correct alignment is nip to seam and not seam to seam.

Displacing the seams of fitted linings should be avoided whenever possible but, if absolutely necessary, the displacements should be minimal – like millimetres not centimetres – because different locations of waist suppression on the cloth and lining could lead to problems. On the body lining for a fitted coat the side seams can be displaced from the hip line down to the hem (Fig. 2.19).

### The sleeve

Patterns for sleeve linings allow for simple modifications because the major part of their length is concealed. These modifications fall into two categories:

(1) *Joins* Most companies accept that joins in the width of a sleeve lining are necessary in order to prevent excessive waste. When the pattern cutter sees that there is an advantage in joining a sleeve pattern, proper patterns for the joined parts should be prepared instead of relying on the marker planner to establish the join line, add seam allowances and mark sewing alignment nips.

(2) *Seam displacements* These are made so that components will efficiently utilise the space available for them. A good example of seam displacements are those which can be applied to a standard, two-piece tailored sleeve. The practical options, shown

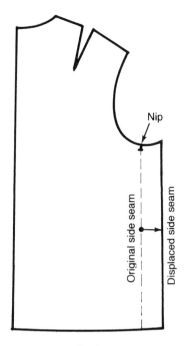

Fig. 2.18. Seam displacement.

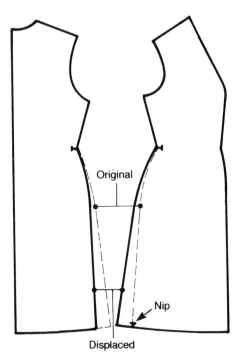

Fig. 2.19. Side seam displacement for fitted lining.

below, all concern displacements of the hindarm seam because displacements of the forearm seam can cause problems due to the differences in seam locations.

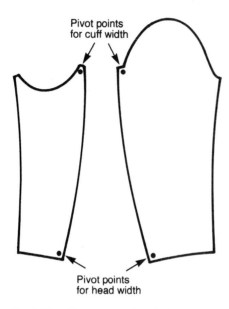

**Fig. 2.20.** Pivot points for hind arm seam displacement.

- Displacing the hind arm seams to increase the width of the top sleeve cuff and decrease that of the under sleeve, or vice versa. The points for this and other pivoting procedures are shown in Fig. 2.20.
- Decreasing the head width of the top sleeve and increasing the width of the related section of the under sleeve. This is also performed by pivoting the pattern from the cuff and the result is shown in Fig. 2.21A.
- Displacing the hind arm seams for their whole length, with the maximum displacement-ment at any one point not exceeding 2.5 cm. This displacement does not have to be uniform for the entire length of the seam but can vary from top to bottom. Fig. 2.21B shows an equi-distant displacement of the hindarm seams which is based on the principle that whatever is reduced from one seam is added exactly to the matching seam. If this type of displacement results in a wider top sleeve and a narrower under sleeve, then there will be an increase in the amount of top sleeve hindarm seam fullness which has to be eased into the hindarm seam of the under sleeve. Two sewing alignment nips along the seam would ensure the correct distribution of the fullness.

As stated at the start of this section, lining patterns do not present many opportunities for modification, but every gain, however small, is a plus for the company.

## COMPUTERISED CUTTING

If the samples and/or bulk work are to be cut by a CAM system, the patterns used for all materials should have a small modification made to their external corners in order to slightly reduce cutting time. The cutting blade of a computer controlled cutting head cannot turn through a sharp

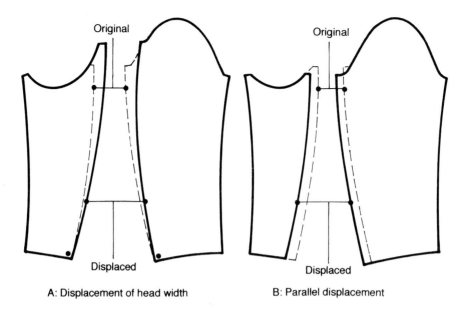

**Fig. 2.21.** Displacement of hind arm seams for sleeve linings.

corner without disturbing a small area of the surrounding material. Consequently, most CAM systems use the following sequence for cutting corners:

(1) The first converging line of the corner is cut to its end.
(2) The blade is then automatically lifted out of the spread and swivelled to the required angle.
(3) It is then plunged back into the spread and starts cutting the second convergent line of the corner. This lift and plunge sequence takes very little time in itself, but when it is used for the numerous sharp corners in a long spread, the time involved can be a significant proportion of the total time required to cut the spread.

The lift and plunge process can be eliminated by slightly rounding off all the sharp external corners of pattern components. As a result, the blade cuts round the corner in an uninterrupted instead of an interrupted action, thus saving time. For components having a seam allowance of 1 cm or more, a coin or disc with a diameter of about 1.5 cm can be used as a template for marking pattern corners. Fig. 2.22 shows an example of a jacket panel with rounded-off external corners.

## TO SUM UP

There is an adage which says that prevention is better than cure, and this is applicable to pattern modifications of all types. The pattern cutter

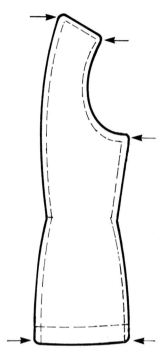

**Fig. 2.22.** Rounding off external corners

should try to anticipate the possible problems regarding materials usage and should incorporate the solutions when preparing the pattern and not when the pattern is being used to prepare a cutting marker. Often a modification to the pattern of a top cloth component would necessitate modifications to lining and fusible components. So there is another relevant saying, something about a stitch in time...

# 3
# Garment Trimmings

In total all the trimmings used for a garment can be a substantial cost item and so their selection and use require careful consideration. There is no point in improving materials utilisation if the savings made are thrown away by using a zip which is two or three centimetres longer than necessary or by using expensive tapes as stay tapes. The professional approach is: sufficient for the intended purpose but no more.

## LININGS

Garment linings have functional and consumer appeal objectives and this section will examine the principles involved, starting with the material itself.

### FIBRE TYPES AND PROPERTIES

Today natural fibres are rarely used to construct linings due to the high cost and some difficulties with imparting a suitable finish to the fabrics. Synthetic fibres are now the most widely accepted for garment linings, and the following describes the main properties of those which have the most widespread use in the clothing industry.

#### Viscose
Viscose is made from cellulose which is derived from wood pulp, and like most other synthetic fibres, it goes through a number of chemical and mechanical processes until the filaments are ready for spinning into yarns. Linings constructed from viscose fibres have strength, lustre, softness and an affinity for dyes.

#### Rayon
Originally rayon was produced as a cheap substitute for silk and the

fibres were known as 'artificial silk'. Rayon linings have similar properties to those of viscose linings but are somewhat weaker.

### Polyamide
Derived from nylon, polyamide produces linings with excellent tensile strength and a relatively high degree of elasticity, and it takes dye-stuffs very well. A drawback with polyamide linings is that some solvents used for dry cleaning can have a detrimental effect on the fabric.

### Polyester
Polyester fibres are closely related to polyamides and linings made from polyester fibres have many similar properties. The first polyester linings had a tendency to soften when pressed with a hot iron, but fibres with a high melting point have since been developed and these withstand regular pressing temperatures.

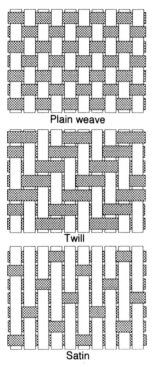

Plain weave

Twill

Satin

**Fig. 3.1.** Lining weave patterns.

Other than some polyamide linings, none of the linings made from these synthetic fibres are harmed by dry cleaning and they can be safely pressed up to a temperature of 170°C. Although some warp knitted linings are available, weaving is the predominant method of construction and three of the basic weaves are shown in Fig. 3.1.

## FUNCTION AND CONSUMER APPEAL

### Function
Garment linings have a number of functional purposes besides their main one which is to cover all or part of the interior surface of a garment. These other functions include:

- As linings have a sheer surface, putting on or taking off the garment is a smooth and simple action.
- Linings help to preserve the shape of skirts and trousers made from loosely constructed or stretchy materials.
- Garments such as dresses, skirts and trousers, made from diaphanous materials, sometimes need 'cover-up' areas. Lining does this job well.
- Some types of outerwear materials have a tendency to cling to the body and this can spoil the silhouette of the garment. A layer of lining between the body of the wearer and the top cloth will usually eliminate this problem.

- Linings are often used to assist in the formation of design features on garments. For example, the difference in lengths between the body shell and the body lining creates the blouson effect. The same principle is also used to create an 'overhang' look on puffed sleeves.

### Consumer appeal

An important factor of consumer appeal is to present a garment whose inside has an attractive appearance. The surface and lustre properties of the lining have a considerable influence on this, and those properties for linings most widely used are:

- *Taffeta*   A crisp fabric woven with a faint warp pattern which produces a shiny surface. These linings are generally piece-dyed which helps to soften them and make them able to withstand normal washing and dry-cleaning processes.
- *Crepe*   Made from specially processed yarns, mostly viscose acetate, the finished surface of this lining has a minute and uniformly crinkled appearance.
- *Satin (sateen)*   This lining is characterised by a smooth and highly lustrous surface and a dull back. Satin is the name of a weave pattern and all-cotton fabrics that were once constructed with this weave pattern were called sateen.

Colour also plays an important role and linings with a woven, printed or embossed pattern can give an extra fillip to a garment. Some large companies incorporate their logo in the weave pattern of their linings.

## THE SELECTION OF LININGS

This is not a simple matter because the properties of different linings overlap to a considerable extent and usually there is little difference in their prices. Apart from considering price, the designer should always work with reputable suppliers who can supply practical proof of the specific properties of their linings. Failing that, a sample length should be requested for trying out in the factory. Very cheap linings should be avoided if possible because if they do not cost much it is likely they are not much of a lining either.

## PRACTICALITIES

### Making-up and testing linings

Lining materials fray easily and should be assembled on a four-thread safety stitch machine. Although thread consumption is greater than on a regular sewing machine, the seam produced is superior.

Irrespective of whether linings are pressed or not before setting, all vertical seam inlays should be pressed to one side. Apart from making the presser's work a little easier when finishing the garment, this helps to prevent 'seam-grin' which could happen if the seam is left to find its own lay direction, or even worse, if the seam is pressed open.

Where the body linings are pressed as one unit with the cloth, the shrinkage factors of the cloth and lining should be checked to verify that the two materials have compatible shrinkage in the width and the length. If the discrepancy is substantial, it would be worth substituting a different lining because working with linings which have excessive shrinkage could lead to complications during production and finishing.

The most practical test for a lined wash-and-wear garment is to wash a garment, using the correct programme, in a domestic washing machine and check the outcome after the garment has been dried and pressed.

Although pinking is sometimes used to finish the hems of skirt seat linings and knee-length trouser linings, these hems will eventually start to fray after moderate wear and cleaning. Consideration should be given to finishing these linings with a double-turn hem in order to prevent fraying and consumer dissatisfaction.

Fleece and quilted linings should be assembled with a five-thread safety stitch machine having a wide bight. The seam produced is stronger and has more extensibility than with a four-thread machine – two properties essential for these types of linings.

### Lining component patterns

Grain line markings are as necessary for linings as they are for top cloth and fusibles. They should match the grain lines of the relative cloth components, although this can be ignored for components such as sleeve linings and linings for skirts and trousers, which are sometimes cut across the piece instead of in the length.

Linings rarely have a pile direction and the up and down arrangement of the components for one size is a standard procedure in the industry. However, it is always safer to check this, especially with sateen, patterned or brushed finish linings. If the lining does have a definite direction, this has to be indicated on the pattern.

The number of nips on lining patterns should be kept to the minimum because every nip is a potential weak spot on the seams. In addition, if the nips fray out before sewing, the assembly operator will have to skirt round the frayed areas by sewing wider seams than those called for.

Despite the fact that linings are sometimes referred to as a secondary material, they have an important functional and consumer appeal role. Therefore the selection, patterns, cutting and making-up of linings should receive the same levels of treatment as those accorded to the top cloth.

## SECONDARY TRIMMINGS

## CLOSURES

Most garments require some form of working parts to open and close them and those parts which are not attached to the garment during its production have to be added in the finishing process. Typical closure systems are discussed here.

## BUTTONS

Buttons and loops were first used to fasten clothing about 600 BC and with the development of the buttonhole in the 13th century buttons became the most widely used closure system for clothing of all types. Throughout the centuries buttons have been made from wood, precious metals and ceramics, many of which are collectors' items today. The modern button is mostly produced from plastic materials such as polyester, acrylic and polyvinyl resins, and they can be designed according to specific requirements.

Garment buttons can serve two purposes:

(1) *Utilitarian*  This refers to buttons which are used to open and close garments and other design features where the wearer requires access combined with an element of security. For example, the hip pocket on trousers or the patch pocket on a safari-styled garment.
(2) *Decorative*  These are buttons which have a purely decorative function and one of the most common forms is on double-breasted garments. Most of the buttons sewn on to the sleeve vents of tailored garments are of decorative value only, although at one time they had a functional purpose.

Figure 3.2 shows the basic types of buttons used for clothing, and how they are attached to garments.

## HOOKS AND EYES

This is a relatively simple closure system which is widely used for zip openings on dresses and blouses made from light-weight materials. Hooks and eyes can be sewn on by hand or by a simple button sewing machine fitted with special clamps for the two working parts.

## HOOKS AND BARS

These are metal closures which are used for trouser and skirt waist bands. Due to their construction, they have to be set whilst the garment is being assembled. If the factory specialises in the production of trousers and/or skirts, the sample room would usually be equipped with a manually operated device for attaching these parts (Fig. 3.3). In the factory these machines are semi-automatic and powered by compressed air systems.

## PRESS STUDS

These can be made from plastic or metal and consist of two working parts, the male and female, which are locked together when subjected to

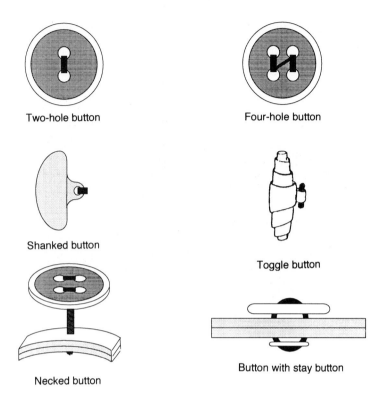

Two-hole button

Four-hole button

Shanked button

Toggle button

Necked button

Button with stay button

**Fig. 3.2.** Buttons and sewing methods.

a slight pressure. It is advisable to set press studs through two plies of material and with knitted fabrics a reinforcement strip between the two plies will prevent distortion.

Like buttons, plastic press studs can be colour matched to materials and often the visible face of metal or plastic studs carries the logo or decal of the producer.

### RIVETS

Whilst these are not closure parts, they are widely used for decorative and reinforcement purposes on denim garments. Rivets require an appropriate device to set them on garments.

## ZIPS

Although slide fasteners, as they were then called, were introduced in 1912, it took about another 20 years before they started to be used for men's and women's clothing. Since then zips have become one of the most extensively used closure methods utilised by the clothing industry. Apart from their functional purposes, zips are also used for decorative

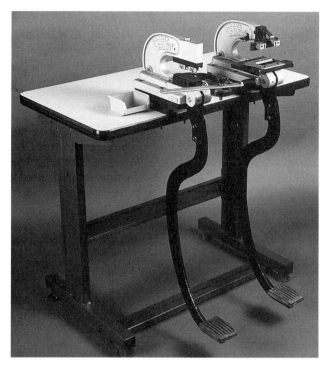

**Fig. 3.3.** Manually operated machine for hooks and bars.

effects or as design features. Zips are a continuous form of closure as against buttons which are intermittent.

## CONSTRUCTION

A regular zip (Fig. 3.4) has the following elements in its construction.

### Tape
The majority of zip tapes are twill woven from 100% polyester, which produces a strong, light-weight tape that does not shrink. Knitted zip tapes are soft and pliable and are mostly used for garments made from knitted fabrics.

### Chain
This element is also referred to as the teeth or scoops and they are made from metal or plastic materials. Metal scoops are stamped out of brass or aluminium and are then clamped on to the beaded edge of the tape. Alternatively, continuous

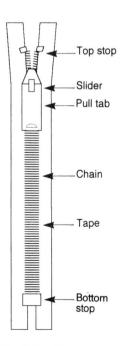

Fig. 3.4. Components of regular zip.

monofilament coils made from nylon or polyester are woven directly into the tape edge. Zips with coiled chains are lighter and more flexible than those with metal chains.

## Slider
The function of the slider is to engage or disengage the opposite sides of the chain as it is moved up or down. The slider can be nonlocking or can have a built-in or semi- or fully-automatic locking action. An automatic locking slider is very dependable although it is bulkier than the other two types.

## Top and bottom stops
These prevent the loss of the slider caused through excessive up or down movement. For zips whose top ends are caught in the waist band seaming, the top stops are often dispensed with as the stitching serves as stops. The bottom stop prevents the zip from being opened to the lower end of the tape and thus jamming the slider.

## Pull tab
This enables the consumer to easily move the slider in the desired direction. Tabs are produced in a great variety of shapes and finishes and are frequently used for decorative purposes.

## ZIP TYPES

There are several types of zips available, which enables the designer to select a zip that is the most suitable for a particular garment or end use. Some of the more commonly used zips are given here.

## Regular type
Used in different lengths for skirts, dresses and other articles of clothing. This zip is usually inserted into a seam and whilst the zip is concealed, the setting stitching shows on the outside of the garment. To set this type of zip, a half presser foot is used which enables the operator to sew close to the chain.

## Invisible zip
So called because the zip and its setting stitching cannot be seen on the right side of the opening. The insertion of this zip requires a special type of presser foot and the setting operation itself is shorter and easier than for a regular zip.

## Separated zip
This type of zip is utilised when the garment can be worn either closed or fully opened. Some typical applications of separated zips are for blousons, parka jackets and zip-out linings.

### Continuous zip

Used for men's trousers and all categories of jeans, continuous zips with an average length of 50 m are wound onto reels with the metal chain closed or separated into left and right sides. This permits each side of the zip to be set onto the respective panels before the crotch seam is closed. The slider and bottom stop are fitted by means of small mechanical devices located in suitable positions along the production line.

Continuous metal zips are cheaper in use than those made to specific lengths as they can be cut to the exact lengths required and there is no need to maintain regular stocks of different lengths or the odds and ends which are bound to accumulate.

### VELCRO

This is one of the trade names for pressure sensitive tapes which have gained widespread acceptance as a closure method for many sportswear articles and items of children's clothing. They consist of two nylon pile tapes, one having a surface of loops and the other a surface of microscopic hooks. When the two pile surfaces are pressed together, the hooks engage the loops creating a closure area the size of the tape. The closure is opened by pulling the two tapes apart.

Pressure sensitive tapes are far more visible and are bulkier than buttons or zips but are simpler to use, especially for cold sportsmen and women or small children. It is not advisable to use these tapes on knitted or looped materials because the strong nylon hooks are liable to damage the fabric.

## SHOULDER PADS

Padding in various forms and on different locations of the body has been used for clothing for about three thousand years, and during the past hundred years or so pads have become a standard shaping medium for the shoulder line. Today, shoulder pads are very much a styling and fashion factor and the designer frequently has to select new shapes and thicknesses.

Pads can be made from foam or layers of non-woven materials around a central foam or fibre layer. For unlined garments a pad covered with polyamide or self-material is generally used, and for lined garments there is no necessity to cover the pad. There are pads specifically for washable garments and for garments which are to be dry-cleaned only. Care should be taken that the pad selected matches up with the cleaning conditions on the care label of the garment. The pads for unlined garments can be attached by a series of tacks made by a button sewing machine or what is called a blind-stitch tacker. For tailored garments, the pads can be sewn in or fused to the shoulder area with small areas of thermoplastic resin positioned on the top layer of the pad.

## TAPES

These are narrow bands of woven fabric which are used for the following purposes in the make-up of clothing:

- *Decorative*   For binding the edges of collars, lapels and flaps, etc.
- *Stretch control*   To prevent seams or edges from stretching during making-up.
- *Finishing*   Sometimes used instead of overlocking on visible seam and hem edges.

Bought-in tapes can be straight or on the bias, depending on their end use, and are available in a large range of widths, colours and finishes. Examples of their use are:

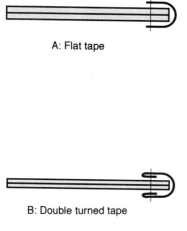

A: Flat tape

B: Double turned tape

**Fig. 3.5.**   Bound edges.

- *Decorative*   These can be sewn to edges with or without turning in the edges of the tape itself. Fig. 3.5A shows the application of a flat tape and Fig. 3.5B the formation of a double turned tape.
- *Stretch control* (Fig. 3.6)   A narrow straight pre-positioned tape is used for this purpose and it is caught into the stitching when the seam or edge is sewn. Armholes, shoulders and sewn fitted waistlines are often taped in this fashion.
- *Finishing*   Bias tapes, cut from the same lining as used for the half-lining

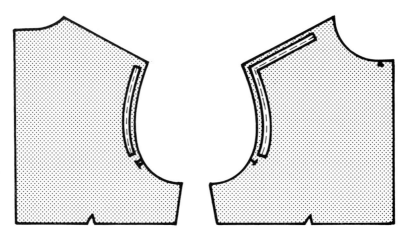

**Fig. 3.6.**   Stay-tape on armhole and shoulder.

of the garment, are used to neaten and finish the edges of the visible seams and hem. This method is sometimes used instead of over-locking for the hems of up-market skirts.

The application of tapes requires special folders and/or guides and pre-ferably a mechanical device which controls the tension and feed of the tape whilst it is being sewn to the garment. Binding the collar and lapels of a garment is a highly skilled and lengthy operation mostly due to the necessity to clean-finish the corners of the lapels and collars. Designers should carefully consider including this type of garment in a collection because they are not very welcome products in the majority of factories.

## TO SUM UP

Garment trimmings have relatively critical functions in the make-up of garments and whilst price is important, so is performance. There are good reasons why some trimmings are seemingly cheap, and their use without prior testing can sometimes result in an expensive boomerang effect.

# PART 2

# GARMENT TECHNOLOGY

# 4

# Introduction to Garment Technology

## INTRODUCTION

Technology has been defined as a technical method of achieving a practical purpose, but its original Greek root meaning is the systematic treatment of an art. This latter meaning is apt for the clothing industry because garment design is a goal oriented art form which requires technology to convert it into a finished product.

Clothing technology is a broad based subject because it combines a number of individual technologies, with each making a specialised contribution to the production of clothing. For the designer and pattern cutter, these technologies can be divided into two groups:

(1) *Need to know* These are the technologies which are directly related to the work of designers and pattern cutters, and it is imperative that they have a practical understanding of the essentials of each particular subject.

(2) *Good to know* This group covers the other technologies which are part of a modern clothing factory but are not of direct concern for designing and pattern cutting. However, the senior members of the design team should have some understanding of these technologies because it will improve their orientation within the working environment.

This chapter will examine the principles of the direct, or need to know, technologies and will demonstrate the considerations involved in their basic applications. There is a great deal of specialised literature available which deals with the good to know group of technologies, and this should be referred to as and when required.

## EXAMPLE

This is a practical example which will illustrate the principles involved.

Two factories have the same operation, which consists of sewing a rectangular label onto a back lining. The label has to be sewn along its four edges at a standard margin, the corners have to be precise and the sewing operation has to be completed with a tack.

*Factory no. 1*   The operator has a regular sewing machine and commences the operation by aligning the label to the lining. Then he or she starts sewing around the label edges, stopping at every corner and making sure, via the hand wheel, that the needle is down before turning through the corner. The length and density of the final tack is determined by the operator.

*Factory no. 2*   Here, the operator has a programmable sewing machine and commences by sewing on one label only. The machine's memory records the number of stitches along each side, the stops at corners with the needle down and when to sew the final tack at a pre-determined length. After checking the first one, the operator can just align the label, press the pedal, turn through the corners and remove the finished work. The machine does the rest.

Quality and time apart, both factories have the same result from this operation, the difference being that in factory no. 1 the operation was completely operator controlled, whilst in factory no. 2, the operator basically fed work to the machine. This very simple example illustrates the difference between using an operator to perform an operation or using technology to perform the major part of an operation.

## BACKGROUND

Clothing technology has a long history which could be said to have started with the discovery of the needle about 18 000 BC. For many centuries only individual garments were made and all the operations involved were executed by hand with the aid of some very primitive tools. Fig. 4.1 shows a pattern layout from *The Tailor's Pattern Book* which was published in 1589. During these times, a typical workshop would consist of the master-craftsman together with some apprentices who were 'serving their time'. Apprentices were obliged to spend seven years of their time learning the craft of tailoring. Fig. 4.2 illustrates some of the tools used for making clothes towards the end of the eighteenth century. Many people made their own clothes and the more affluent families would employ a resident or visiting seamstress.

The production of clothing was essentially a domestic industry dominated by local craft guilds who first appeared in England during the thirteenth century. The absolute control of the craft guilds, who dictated

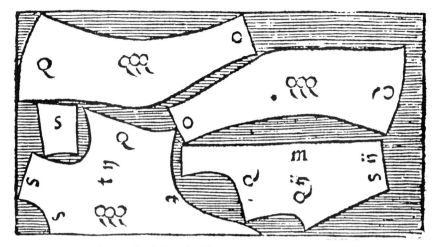

**Fig. 4.1.** Pattern layout for ladies doublet, circa AD 1590.

all the terms and conditions of making clothes, lasted until about the end of the eighteenth century, when the first glimmers of the Industrial Revolution started to appear. It took until the middle of the nineteenth century for clothing production to start becoming industrialised, but once it started it grew swiftly, made possible to a large extent by the technological advances in machinery and equipment, for example:

- *Sewing machines* Although hand-operated, domestic sewing machines (Fig. 4.3) had been on the market since the 1830s, industrial machines were nonexistent at that time. It did not take long, however, for the machine manufacturers to produce sturdy, pedal driven sewing machines which could sew 20 stitches a minute. By the end of the nineteenth century there were electrically powered machines capable of more than 200 stitches a minute.
- *Cutting* Garments had always been cut by shears or slot-knives, but when bulk cutting became required, these tools made it a long and laborious process. The introduction of a band-knife cutting machine in 1860 paved the way for cutting spreads of materials.
- *Spreading* Manually powered and operated spreading machines started coming into use during the 1880s.
- *Buttonholes* A machine for sewing eyelet buttonholes was patented by the Reece Company in 1900, although some early versions had been around since the 1860s. (Fig. 4.4).
- *Pressing* Don Hoffman developed the first steam pressing machine in 1905.

From the end of the nineteenth century until the start of World War II in 1939, many technological advances were made, but the most significant developments have been made since the end of World War II in 1945 and are greater than all those made during the previous recorded history of

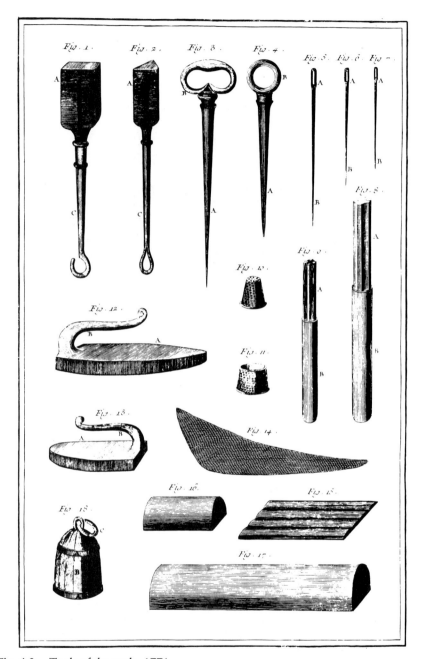

**Fig. 4.2.**  Tools of the trade, 1771.

making clothes. There are many reasons for this period of accelerated progress since 1945, and four of the most relevant are:

- During World War II, people all over the world had been deprived of the opportunity to purchase clothes due to the shortage of materials and labour. After the war there was enormous demand for all types of

**Fig. 4.3.** Singer sewing machine, 1854 (Science Museum/Science and Society Picture Library).

clothing, but the capabilities then available were insufficient to meet the ever increasing requirements.

- The traditional clothing materials such as wool and cotton were in extremely short supply as well as being very expensive. Synthetic fabrics soon filled the gap, but these new materials required different making-up technologies.
- Skilled labour was scarce and methods of production had to be developed which would reduce the reliance on an expensive and relatively diminished labour force. The only answer was the division of labour into skilled, semiskilled and unskilled categories. While this drastically reduced the training time for semiskilled and unskilled labour, there was still the problem of not having machinery and equipment suitable for this new situation. The basic need was for machinery that did not require the input and control of a skilled operator, but had many of the skills needed built into the machine itself.
- The production of sewing machinery had almost ceased during the war and many of the factories had been destroyed. This meant almost starting from scratch for the machinery producers who wanted to recommence their pre-war activities. During the war, in other industries, many advances had been made in metallurgy, instru-

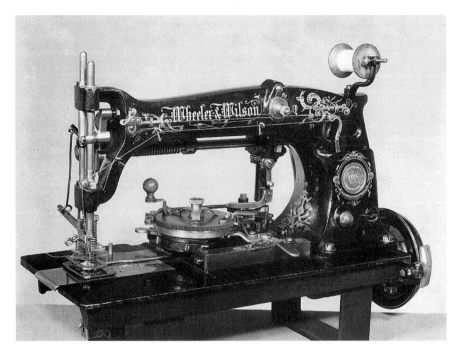

**Fig. 4.4.** Buttonhole machine, 1870 (Science Museum/Science and Society Picture Library).

mentation and control systems, and these, combined with input from the clothing industry, provided machinery manufacturers with the bases for developing new concepts.

These four reasons provide the total picture of why the development of clothing technology really took off in the years following 1945. Some of the more notable advances in clothing technology during the 50 years after 1945 are:

- The introduction of fusibles, together with their particular textile, resin and engineering technologies.
- Sewing machines with electronically controlled needle positioning, thread cutting, back-tacking mechanisms and memory sewing systems.
- Designing, pattern making, grading and marker planning by means of CAD systems.
- Microprocessor or computer controlled production machinery and equipment.
- High speed cutting via CAM systems.
- Programmable spreading and pressing machines.
- Computer driven materials handling systems.
- Robotic and manoeuvrer systems.

In addition, computerised systems for all planning, control, administration and financial management have been introduced. At the time of writing, the objectives of a modern clothing factory are to combine the separate computerised technology concerned with production and management into one overall system. This concept is called computer integrated manufacturing (CIM) and there is no doubt that CIM systems will gradually become an essential element in the infrastructure of clothing factories.

## FOR THE DESIGNER AND PATTERN CUTTER

All clothing factories have a specific technological capability which has been built around the production of a particular category of garments. The levels of technology vary from factory to factory, even between those producing the same garment at similar time standards. Irrespective of the levels of operation, it is essential that the designer and pattern cutter both work according to the given framework and when possible, exploit it to its fullest extent.

With regard to the applications of technology, for the designer it is mainly a question of what the factory can do and knowing the extent of the permissible variations. The pattern cutter also has to know what the factory can do, but also to know how it is done and what is required to do it. These factors have to be incorporated into the garment pattern, plus all the standard technological processes which the average garment undergoes during making-up.

Where does the interaction of the designer and pattern cutter with the factory's technology start? It starts with both of them learning and understanding the factory's technological resources and capabilities. This is vital for a full and efficient involvement on their part. There is nothing more frustrating for all concerned than to invest time in developing a design and pattern and then discovering that the factory is not equipped to perform one or more of the operations required.

Whether the company is prepared to invest in a new item of machinery or equipment is a commercial decision based on whether the acquisition will have a restricted use during one season only or whether it has a range of other possible applications. If the item is going to be limited to an unknown number of garments during one season only, it is back to the drawing board for the designer and pattern cutter.

The sample room is usually equipped with machinery which covers regular operations only, because it is costly to have high-tech machines which are only used occasionally in the sample room. When there are new samples which require operations beyond the scope of the sample room machinery, these operations should be performed in the factory and not 'faked-up' in the sample section. The factory is where the garments will be produced and special operations should be validated there and nowhere else. It is important that the sample room produces garments which incorporate the relevant technology, and this means working hand in hand with the factory. It is possible to improvise many special operations in the sample room with time, pins, basting thread and skilled labour, but this is not the situation in the factory. So the people responsible have to ensure that sample garments can be mass-produced by utilising as much as possible of the available technology.

## TO SUM UP

The applications of technology demand methods and techniques, and both of these require a specialised and systematic approach. This is also a desirable approach to technology for designers and pattern cutters.

# 5
# Sample Cutting

## PREPARATION FOR CUTTING

### INTRODUCTION

For all practical purposes the sample room is the research and
development department of a clothing factory, and one of the technical
subjects which has to be examined is cutting. Before a sample garment can
be mass-produced its practicability and efficiency as regards cutting have
to be ensured; it is irresponsible to present the cutting room with unre-
solved problems. It is worth bearing in mind that if something does not
work in the sample room, it certainly will not work in the cutting room.

### GARMENT PATTERN AND FABRIC

There are four preparatory processes which have to be carried out before
starting to cut samples, and they deal with:

(1)  *The pattern*  As a medium of communication and as a production
     tool
(2)  *Grain lines*  Establishing the linear relationship between the gar-
     ment pattern and the cloth
(3)  *Pile direction*  How this influences pattern component arrange-
     ments
(4)  *Fabric pattern*  What has to be taken into account.

Part of the pattern cutter's job is to perform processes (1) and (2), and the
sample cutter applies the remaining two when preparing the cutting
marker for a particular fabric. Each of these processes is now discussed in
turn.

## (1) THE PATTERN

The pattern is the primary link between design and production and so must communicate accurately with all the functions that have to use the pattern. These functions are pattern grading, marker planning and sewing, and the pattern has to clearly and precisely convey the information necessary to perform each of these operations. This information is conveyed by numbers, marks, nips and notches, etc, and *not* by written instructions. New sample patterns always require some explanation, but there should be no necessity for verbal or written working instructions when it comes to production. The pattern should tell the complete story to all concerned.

There should be a pattern for every component to be cut. Marker planners or cutters are not expected to be pattern makers or pattern guessers, therefore pattern sets must be complete in every respect. Each pattern part must be marked on both sides with grain lines and direction indicators. Patterns should be paired when the garment is to be cut from open rather than folded fabric. Two practical methods of pairing patterns are by marks and by colour:

- *By marks* (Fig. 5.1A).   Cut pairs for each component and mark an X on one side only of each of the two components when they are in a paired position. The blank sides indicate correct pairing, as do the marked sides.
- *By colour* (Fig. 5.1B).   This method requires a pattern card with a different colour on each side. Staple two pieces of the card together with the same colour inside, and then cut out the components. Pairing is achieved when the same colour shows for a pair of the same component.

Patterns for asymmetrical garments should be prepared for positioning

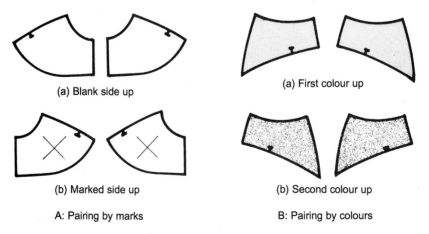

<table>
<tr><td>(a) Blank side up</td><td>(a) First colour up</td></tr>
<tr><td>(b) Marked side up</td><td>(b) Second colour up</td></tr>
<tr><td>A: Pairing by marks</td><td>B: Pairing by colours</td></tr>
</table>

**Fig. 5.1.**   Pattern pairing methods.

on the right side of the cloth only. A simple method to ensure the correct face-up positioning is to mark the reverse side of the components with a large X.

Every pattern piece must be clearly identified as regards style number, garment type, the material for which the pattern is intended and the number of components in a set for a particular material, i.e. cloth, lining and fusibles. A simple and standard method is to use a rubber stamp, an example of which is illustrated in Fig. 5.2.

| GERLIN FASHIONS LTD | | |
|---|---|---|
| Style number | | *6108* |
| Comp. number | | *EJ4 ø 6B* |
| Garment type | | *Jacket* |
| Size | Home | |
| | Export | *42R* |
| Material | | *Lining* |
| Pieces in set | | *6* |
| Component | | *Back* |

Fig. 5.2. Pattern identification stamp.

## (2) GRAIN LINES

This refers to the positioning of pattern components in relation to the true length of the fabric. For woven materials this line is the warp threads and for knitted fabrics it is the wales.

A garment will hang in a direct relationship to the grain directions of the body components. If the grain lines are incorrect, the finished garment will have a distorted appearance which cannot be rectified. This also applies to sleeves which are sewn to the body, such as inset, raglan and dolman. In many instances wavy hemlines are also a direct result of off-grain components. Therefore it is essential that each pattern component is marked with a grain line on both sides for its complete length (Fig. 5.3). The grain line is also often used as a datum line when digitising patterns for computerised grading.

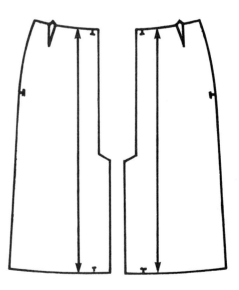

Fig. 5.3. Example of grain lines (marked on both sides of pattern).

As a general guide, the grain lines for main components are:

- *Fronts*  Parallel to the centre front.
- *Backs*  Parallel to the centre back.

- *Sleeves* On or parallel to the true centre line.
- *Lapel facings* The grain line runs parallel to the edge of the lapel section. If this positioning produces an acute bias angle on the lower part of the facing, it is sometimes permitted to make a join across the facing between the top and second buttonhole
- *Patch pockets* Relative to their position on the front; the grain line is parallel to that of the front.
- *Inset pockets* For piped, welted and similar types of inset pockets, the grain line runs along the length of the pocket piece or pieces.
- *Top collars* On the centre back line of the collar.
- *Under collars* These can be omnidirectional because the grain line of the fusible used for this component is the controlling grain line. It serves no practical purpose to insist that under collars are cut on the true bias whilst top collars are cut according to the straight grain.
- *Other parts* Generally, the grain lines can be derived from the grain line of the component on which the part is located.

Some typical examples of grain line markings are shown in Fig. 5.4.

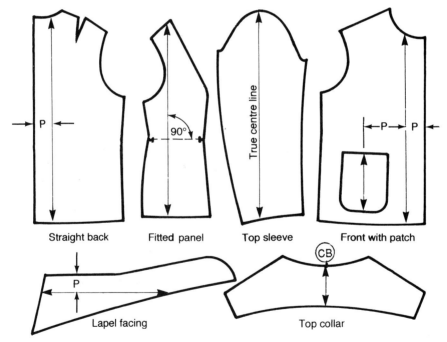

**Fig. 5.4.** Examples of grain line marks (P = parallel to).

Whilst there are firm principles involved in the determination of grain lines, sometimes design features and practical considerations have to be given preference, especially with checked fabrics. For example, matching a patch pocket on a check material demands a considerable amount of work in cutting and sewing. The designer could consider cutting the pocket on the true bias which would greatly reduce the difficulties of this operation. It is sometimes necessary to make practical compromises and the designer has to be prepared to weigh up the pros and cons of alternative courses of action. A little common sense goes a long way, especially when labour costs are concerned.

## (3) PILE DIRECTION

This describes the lay (direction), length and density of the protruding fibres on the surface of the right side of the cloth. The question regarding pile is to what extent it influences the positioning of pattern components on the cloth whilst observing the grain line markings. All fabrics have a pile factor and for practical purposes they can be grouped under three headings:

(1)  *One-way* (Fig. 5.5A)  On these fabrics there is a prominent pile which lays in one direction only. Typical examples of this type of cloth are corduroy, velvet and mohair. Due to the very definite pile lay, the components of all the sizes in a cutting marker must be positioned in one direction only.

(2)  *Two-way* (Fig. 5.5B)  This type of cloth is one of the most widely used in the clothing industry because the pile factor allows for higher utilisation than with one-way fabrics. Whilst these cloths do have a pile factor it is minimal, and this permits the positioning of components for each size in opposite directions. This method of positioning patterns in a cutting marker is often referred to as 'one-up, one-down'. Fig. 5.6 shows two markers planned according to different pile conditions.

(3)  *No-pile*  Although this heading is a misnomer, it refers to materials which have a virtually negligible pile factor. This enables components for

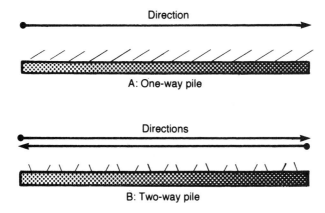

**Fig. 5.5.**  Pile directions.

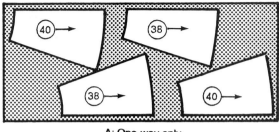

A: One-way only

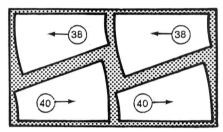

B: One-up, one-down

**Fig. 5.6.**  Markers according to pile direction.

one size to be positioned in opposite directions. Fabrics for blouses, shirts and underwear are examples of this widely used group.

### Preparing the pattern

To ensure the correct positioning of the garment pattern within the cutting marker, every component has to be marked on both sides with direction indicators. Under most circumstances these indicators can be marked on the grain line and Fig. 5.7 shows the application of this method for the alternative positioning procedures. It is worth bearing in mind that garment patterns are not always used for one fabric exclusively, so every new fabric which is to be cut from a previously used production pattern must be checked for its pile factor and the pattern markings changed if necessary.

### (4) FABRIC PATTERN

This refers to the form of the pattern on the right side of the cloth, and has three aspects:

(1)  *One-way* (Fig. 5.8)   This is where the pattern form dictates that the garment patterns for every size in the cutting marker must be positioned in one direction only. For example, if the motif on a printed fabric is an upright human figure then it is preferable that the figures stand on their feet and not on their heads.

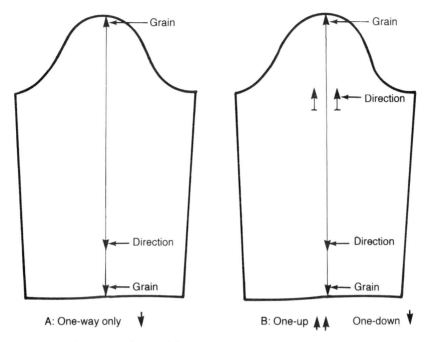

**Fig. 5.7.** Marking grain line and direction.

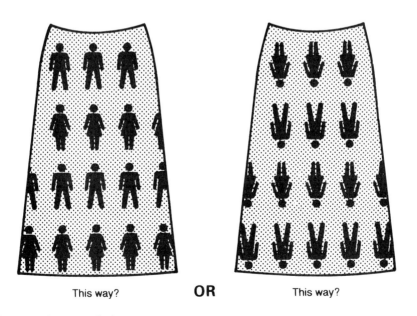

**Fig. 5.8.** One-way cloth pattern.

(2) *Two-way* (Fig. 5.9) This type of pattern form has a definite direction but it is not sufficiently dominant to warrant one-way only positioning. In most cases the pattern components for each size can be positioned one-up, one down, but this decision has to be carefully evaluated.

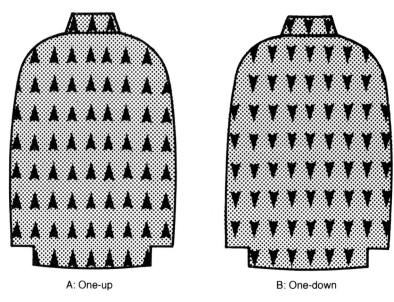

A: One-up        B: One-down

**Fig. 5.9.** Optional two-way cloth pattern.

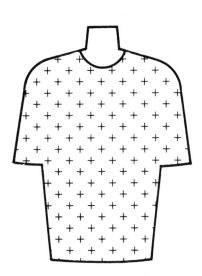

**Fig. 5.10.** Non-directional cloth pattern.

Consider the situation in a retail shop where two garments of the same style and fabric, but cut in opposite directions, are hanging side by side on a display rail. Would the difference in cloth pattern direction be easily noticeable or would it be sufficiently 'blurred' to be of little consequence? There are no rules for this subject; that a large element of objective judgement is called for.

(3) *Non-directional* (Fig. 5.10) This type of pattern form has no definite directions and, subject to the pile factor, pattern components for one size can be positioned in either length direction.

Patterned fabrics also include checks

and stripes and these will be examined in the final section of this chapter.

## TO SUM UP

Cutting is an operation where severe mistakes are sometimes very difficult or even impossible to rectify. Sample garments are usually cut from short sample lengths and if they are spoiled by a serious mistake, obtaining a replacement in time could be difficult. There are no cast-iron methods of preventing cutting mistakes, but the possibilities of mistakes occurring can be greatly reduced by the thorough and correct preparation of the garment pattern prior to cutting the sample garment.

## MARKER PLANNING

## INTRODUCTION

To cut a sample garment, the pattern components have to be economically arranged according to their grain lines and the pile direction of the fabric which is to be cut. The regular form of this arrangement is a rectangle with the short side equivalent to the net width of the fabric and the long side the length required to contain the pattern components. The drawing of this arrangement is a cutting marker (Fig. 5.11) and when starting to prepare markers, there are a number of procedures which have to be followed. This starts by determining the net width of the cloth

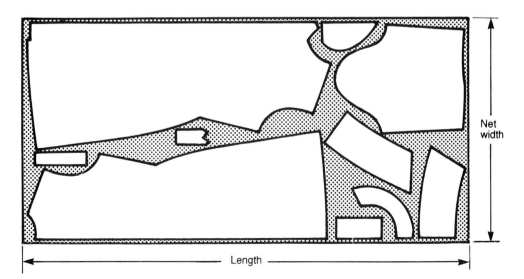

**Fig. 5.11.** Example of single width marker (pile direction disregarded).

to be cut, which can be easily done but there are some practical considerations involved.

## NET WIDTH

This is sometimes called the cutable width and both terms refer to the width remaining after the measurements of the two selvedges have been deducted from the gross width of the fabric. With most woven materials the selvedges are constructed from stronger warp threads than those used for the fabric itself. As the selvedge is stronger it is also thicker and very likely to have a different shrinkage factor from that of the fabric. It is not advisable to include this type of selvedge in garments.

The selvedges of many light weight woven materials are constructed from the same warp threads as the fabric, and this enables the selvedge to be utilised if needed. Often the selvedge is used for the inside edge of facings on shirts and blouses, which is a saving in cutting and overlocking.

Most knitted fabrics are produced in tubular form and are then slit open in their length. As the slitting process is not always 100% accurate, some allowance has to be made for possible irregularities in the width. In addition, the edges could have slight damages caused by the pin-plates or clips which hold the fabric in position when it is being fed through a stentering machine to stabilise the finished width of the fabric.

Flat-knit fabrics have finished edges, but they also go through the stentering process, which could leave small damages along the edges. The practical conclusion is that the edges of all open knitted fabrics should be carefully examined in order to determine the correct net width of the fabric.

## PRINCIPLES OF MARKER PLANNING

### MANUAL PLANNING

There are no fixed rules for the manual planning of cutting markers because in the main this process relies on the perceptual sense of the planner and the ability to 'see' the best interlocking combination of the pattern components. Nevertheless, there are a number of principles which can be applied.

Before starting to plan the marker there are some preparatory procedures to perform:

- The pattern set should be checked to ascertain that it contains the correct number of components for the material which is to be cut
- If the marker is for open cloth, the pattern set should be verified for correct pairing
- Each component must be clearly marked with grain lines and direction indicators
- The direction indicators should be checked against the fabric itself

- Net width has to be established
- It would help if the main matching points for checked materials are marked on the relevant pattern components
- This also applies to the symmetry requirements for checked and striped materials.

When these procedures have been completed the planner or cutter can start the actual planning of the marker, incorporating some or all of the following guidelines:

- If the marker is being planned on marker paper, the first stage is to mark the net width for the estimated length, and a starting line at one end. When the marker is being planned directly on the cloth, one end should be ripped across the weft line so as to show whether the cloth is laying straight or otherwise.
- The largest components should be positioned first and where possible the smaller parts are fitted into the remaining spaces.
- Similarly curved lines should be interlocked when possible (Fig. 5.12A).
- The same principle applies to the positioning of angled and straight sections which have corresponding forms (Fig. 5.12B).
- When there is a permissible amount of tilt from the grainline, care should be taken that two seams which are to be joined are tilted by the same amount.
- The garment cannot be cut precisely if interlocked parts, especially curved sections, are butted too closely together.
- A tight (efficient) marker is characterised by the small amounts of 'daylight' showing between the components.

## COMPUTER AIDED MARKER PLANNING

CAD systems are widely used in sample rooms when large numbers of new sample markers have to be produced continuously. Most of these

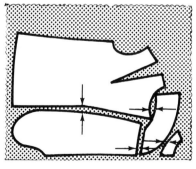
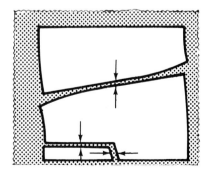

A: Interlocking curved sections    B: Interlocking straight sections

**Fig. 5.12.** Interlocking pattern components.

systems have two alternative modes of operation and the choice between
them is dictated by the amount of time available for planning and the
accessibility of the system during the regular working day. Before
starting to plan by either mode, a number of constraints have to be input
to the system and these include net width, pile direction, distance
between components and the permissible amount of tilt. In addition, the
matching points for checked materials also have to be input when
necessary. The two modes of operation are interactive and automatic:

- *Interactive*  This is a two-way electronic communication function
  between the planner and the system which enables the operator to
  plan markers with the aid of a computer. During the planning process
  the system automatically applies the relevant constraints and also
  indicates to the planner the length of the marker at any given stage. As
  the system controls all the important details, the planner can concentrate on efficient positioning and reiterations.
- *Automatic*  When using this mode, another constraint has to be
  input: the maximum permissible length of the particular marker to be
  planned. The system plans the markers without any manual inter-
  vention and automatically rejects markers which exceed the permissible length. This length is an estimate based on experience and can
  sometimes lead to the excess usage of materials, but if marker production is more important than a little wastage, the waste has to be
  accepted. Another benefit of the automatic mode is that markers can
  be planned overnight without operators being present, thus freeing
  the system and staff for other productive purposes during the regular
  working day.

## MARKER MAKING

If a CAD system is not used in the sample room, the markers have to be
prepared manually. For this two methods can be employed: chalk and
paper.

### Chalk
This is the simplest and cheapest method but it generally produces
inaccurate markers because of the following drawbacks:

- Chalked lines have a tendency to be thick, and thick lines are not
  conducive to accurate cutting.
- Wax chalk marks remain on the cloth for a reasonable length of time
  but pipe-clay marks can wholly or partially disappear if the marker is
  handled often. This could necessitate re-marking or sometimes a little
  dubious guesswork on the part of the cutter.
- Using undue pressure on the chalk marking can cause some slight
  distortion of the marked lines, which does not help with the maintenance of accuracy.

Chalked markers have no real place in a sample room with aspirations towards precision cutting.

## Paper
A very accurate method of making markers is to mark the planned pattern arrangement on paper with a fine pen or sharp pencil. There are printed papers specially produced for this purpose, and the two most generally used are:

- *Spot and cross* (Fig. 5.13)  One side of this paper is printed with alternate spot and cross symbols at 2.5 cm spacings in width and length. This print pattern provides the marker planner with very accurate guides for length, width and true bias positioning of components.
- *One-to-five* (Fig. 5.14)  This marker paper has a print pattern of alternate rows of the letters A to E and the numbers 1 to 5, all at 2.5 cm square spacings. The alphanumeric format of this paper gives the planner a high level of visual accuracy control for the placement of patterns.

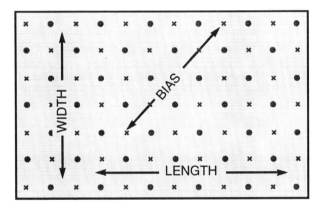

**Fig. 5.13.**  Spot and cross marker paper.

The advantages of using paper markers are accuracy, the retention of markings and the ease of duplication through wide carbon paper or NCR marker paper.

   When completed the paper marker has to be securely affixed to the cloth and there are several methods used for this:

(1)  *Staples*  This method requires a long-arm stapler which can reach within the marker without distorting the lay of the cloth and marker. The staples are positioned in the waste areas of the marker so as to avoid damaging the fabric.
(2)  *Contact adhesive*  This is sprayed onto the cloth and on the

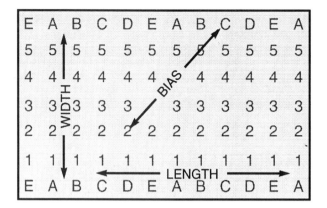

**Fig. 5.14.** One-to-five marker paper.

underside of the marker. Slight pressure is sufficient to bond the two layers securely.

(3) *Heat-seal adhesive* The reverse side of the marker paper is coated with an adhesive and the marker is secured to the cloth by pressing the paper with a light domestic iron, or a large heated plate specially manufactured for this purpose.

The materials used to affix markers are water soluble and they dissolve when the garment is pressed with steam. There could be a problem of residual staining on very fine materials and this should be checked for before deciding how to affix the marker.

## MATERIALS USAGE

The sample room cannot provide exact figures for materials usage because the amount of material actually required for a garment is somewhat more than the length of the sample marker. Most factories work on a fixed percentage of the marker length, which covers the losses from spreading waste, the elimination of defects, remnants, etc. In practical terms this calculation belongs more to the costing clerk or department than it does to the sample room. What the sample room has to ensure is that:

(1) The sample marker is as efficient as possible
(2) The cost of the material used is within the planned framework for the particular category of garments.

There are factories which require only a fairly accurate estimate from the sample room because they derive materials requirements from multisize markers which are far more efficient than the single-size markers.

The designer and pattern cutter should also be involved in the marker planning process, and through joint consultation with the marker planner, each marker has to be examined to see whether materials usage can be reduced by pattern modifications. Marker planning is the key factor in materials costs and every centimetre saved is a potential advantage for the company.

## CUTTING

Single sample garments can be cut with regular shears or by powered scissors (Fig. 5.15) which are just as accurate as shears but are faster and require less physical effort on the part of the cutter. Computerised cutting systems have been developed for single-ply cutting and these are used in sample rooms where large numbers of samples have to be cut continuously.

If the marker is planned on the CAD system it is transferred to the cutting system without the need to plot markers. These systems cut very precisely and the cutting speed is eight to ten times faster than manual methods. Such a system is a substantial investment but a viable one when sample garments have to be produced in large quantities.

**Fig. 5.15.** Powered scissors.

## TO SUM UP

Marker planning is an important pivotal activity because of its direct influence on material costs, cutting accuracy and sewing efficiency. The clothing industry adage which says that the garment is born on the cutting table is very true for the sample room, and no less true for the factory.

## CUTTING CHECKS AND STRIPES

## INTRODUCTION

Checks and stripes are called, with good reason, problem materials because of the many difficulties involved in their cutting and sewing. This is especially true when there are bold patterns and full matching and symmetry are necessary. There is no one single proven method of cutting these materials because cloth patterns and garment patterns vary considerably, and there is always the possibility that the cloth has been distorted during its finishing processes. However, there are some basic techniques and approaches which can be used and they relate to:

(1) The fabric pattern itself
(2) The suitability of the garment pattern
(3) Where to match the cloth pattern
(4) When symmetry is necessary.

The following examples assume that grain lines and pile directions are adhered to, and Fig. 5.16 illustrates the main terms used.

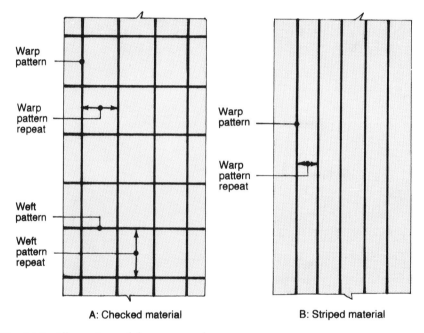

**Fig. 5.16.**  Illustrations of the terms used.

## FABRIC PATTERN

This is where it all starts because a decision has to be made as to whether the fabric pattern is:

- Bold enough to warrant full matching
- Sufficiently prominent to require partial matching
- Indistinct, and can therefore be safely ignored.

The reasoning is as follows.

## FULL MATCHING

This is necessary when there is a conspicuous pattern which, if not matched, would create a visual dissonance on the finished garment. For checked materials and those with prominent weft stripes, this means that the body and sleeves have to be matched all round the garment. These fabrics also require symmetrical elements and sometimes a degree of matching of the warp line pattern.

## PARTIAL MATCHING

This applies mainly to heavily warp striped materials, such as a regularly spaced solid chalk stripe. There are standard features on garments made from these materials which require matching and symmetry and the grain lines play a very important role.

## NO MATCHING

If checked or striped materials have a very small pattern motif, there is usually no need for matching or symmetry. What is essential with this type of material is that the grain lines must be strictly observed.

Examples and explanations of matching symmetry are given later in this section.

# THE GARMENT PATTERN

When planning to make sample garments in checked or striped materials, the designer has to consider whether the intended designs are suitable for the selected materials.

A fabric with a strong pattern is usually the dominant design feature of a garment and, in effect, it is the fabric which is being sold and not seaming and decoration. Therefore it follows that prominent cloth patterns should retain as much of their continuity as possible and not be broken up by seams, darts, etc. In practical terms this means that garment patterns for these materials should contain the minimum number of components which require matching and/or symmetry. A garment design which has a simple assembly will greatly help to minimise the costs of cutting and sewing.

# MATCHING

Although there are a number of similarities in matching checked or striped materials, it is best to consider them individually.

## CHECKS

Cutting these materials has to combine the matching of both the warp and weft patterns and the first question is, where does it start? The size of the warp and weft pattern repeats are the determining factors.

### The start

As an example, a typical travel garment would usually have a bulky collar and lapel and the total width of the collar at the centre back is the stand height plus the fall depth. Assuming that the stand height is 5 cm and the fall depth is 9 cm, the fall section of the collar would overlap the back neck seam by 4 cm. With bold patterns it would be preferable to have the weft pattern line running across the centre of the fall section and not positioned close to the outside edge, in order to avoid the possible distortion of the pattern line by irregularities in sewing or pressing. Accordingly, the distance to the next weft stripe down would need to be the measurement of the weft repeat (Fig. 5.17). As the position of the first weft stripe on the back has been determined, this will then provide the starting point for matching the front and sleeve.

The same technique can also be used for small weft patterns and close repeats, but care should be taken that the net hem line is not positioned on, or close to, the weft pattern line, so that there is no danger of the cloth pattern line being broken up by mistakes in turning-up or pressing the hem.

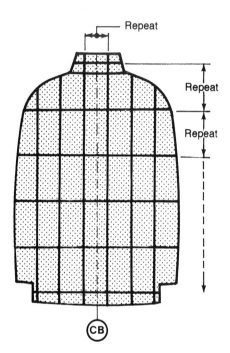

**Fig. 5.17.**  Check pattern matching on back.

### Sleeves

Irrespective of whether one-piece or split sleeves are being cut, the top section, or visible part, of both sleeves has to match the body. If the sleeve has been correctly constructed vis-a-vis the armhole, the weft matching would start a short distance above the bust line and continue up to the shoulder (Fig. 5.18). The objective is to achieve a continuous line around the body and sleeve head even though there are armhole seams.

If the top section of the sleeve is in one piece, the centre line of this

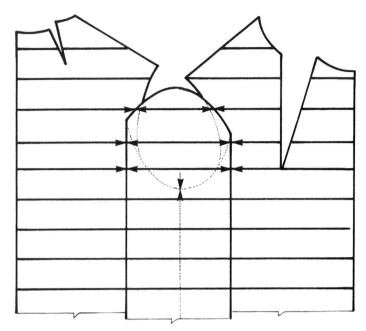

**Fig. 5.18.** Weft pattern alignment for body and sleeve.

section should be positioned on the centre of a warp repeat. For centrally split sleeves such as raglans or dolmans, both the *net* centre seams must be positioned on the centre of a warp repeat. When combined, these matching techniques for the warp and weft patterns ensure an unbroken cloth pattern on the top section of the sleeve.

### Top collars and backs

The objective of this matching technique is to maintain an unbroken warp pattern down the back, from the crease line of the top collar through to the garment's hem.

If the back is cut in one piece (whole back), the centre back line has to be positioned on the centre of a warp repeat, as is the centre back line of the top collar. Where the back has a centre back seam, the net seam line is also positioned on the centre of a warp repeat (Fig. 5.19) and the centre

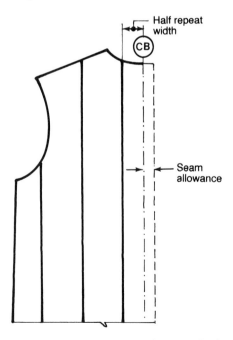

**Fig. 5.19.** Stripe alignment for centre back with seam.

line of the collar is positioned accordingly. Both these instances require that the top collar is both warp and weft matched.

### Other components

Other components have to be dealt with on an individual basis and the designer should always consider how the matching requirements can be simplified without affecting the design integrity. The matching of the lapel facings for checked materials is covered later in this chapter in the section on symmetry.

### STRIPES

Apart from special design features, the matching of warp striped materials is mainly concerned with matching the top collar to the back, and with alignment of the front edges. The other matching requirements for striped materials are those connected with symmetry, dealt with in the next section.

The techniques for matching the centre back section of the top collar to the back are exactly the same as those used for matching the warp pattern of checked materials. The objective is also the same – to ensure the pattern continuity of the entire back section of the garment.

All types of sewn-in sleeves should be positioned according to their grain lines, and pockets such as welts and patches should be matched in the area on which they are located. With patch pockets and flaps on fitted garments, it is not possible to match the entire length of the mouth of the pocket with the body because of waist darts or shaped seams. Under these circumstances, it is acceptable to match only the first two or three stripes from the front edge of the pocket.

What is important for striped materials is that the grain line positioning on the cloth should be as precise as possible. It does not help the appearance of a finished garment if the stripes on adjoining parts give the impression that they are going in opposing directions.

## SYMMETRY

As the majority of garments are symmetrical it follows that the pattern of a material should be positioned symmetrically on the garment. The objective of symmetrical positioning is to make sure that there is a correspondence of the cloth pattern on opposite sides of the garment, i.e. front to front, lapel to lapel, pocket to pocket, etc.

### STRIPES

The main feature requiring symmetry on garments made from striped materials is the top collar together with the lapel facing (Fig. 5.20).

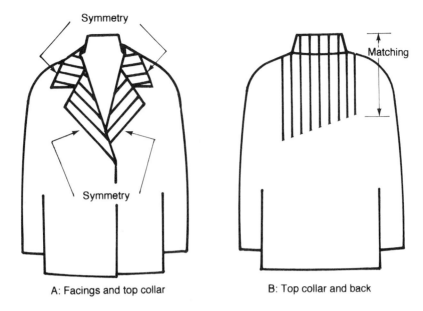

**Fig. 5.20.** Symmetry and matching for stripes.

## Top collar

The positions of the stripes at the collar ends is a consequence of the positioning of the collar centre back line, and the two collar ends have to be exactly the same. As the collar stripes are at a different angle from those of the facing seam, they cannot be matched along this seam.

## Lapel facing

The stripe on the fabric should be parallel to the edge of the lapel, and the distance from the edge to the stripe has to be the same on both sides. It is advisable not to position the stripe too close to the edge in order to prevent it from being broken up by incorrect sewing or pressing.

## CHECKS

Achieving symmetry with checked materials is complicated by the fact that the weft pattern also has to be taken into account. Again, the main feature requiring symmetry is the top collar and the lapel facing and the same principles as with striped materials can be applied to checked materials, with the proviso that the weft stripes on the collar ends and facing are also symmetrical (Fig. 5.21). Components such as patch pockets must be symmetrical irrespective of how they are to be matched.

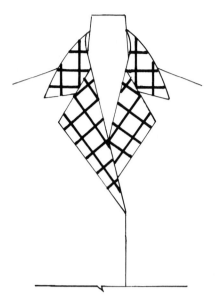

**Fig. 5.21.** Symmetry of collar and facings for check materials.

# SKIRTS AND TROUSERS

So far, in the sections dealing with matching and symmetry, examples have concentrated on body garments because these garments contain all the features necessary to demonstrate the techniques involved. But the clothing industry does not just produce body garments, it also produces skirts and trousers and sometimes these two garments are made from checked and striped materials.

## SKIRTS

Pleats of all kinds are a customary design feature for skirts. When used in designs for checked or striped skirts they can create a problem for the cutting room. Every pleat line on the skirt demands the following procedures:

- Strict observance of grain lines
- Symmetry of the pleat openings, apart from that for the front and back
- Maintenance of the fabric design continuity in the areas containing pleats.

When taken together these procedures are costly, and whenever possible the necessity to use them should be minimal.

As with body garments mentioned earlier, if materials have prominent patterns these are the central design feature of the shirt, and the fabric is the selling focus, not pleats and seaming. So the conclusion for the designer is to keep it simple, because if it is simple it is also quick.

## TROUSERS

As a rule, apart from fabrics and colours, trouser designs concentrate on silhouette and fitting rather than on seaming and decorative effects. This means that matching and symmetry are relatively simple for the cutting room. Grain lines have to be observed, and for checks the pattern on the leg seams has to be matched and the pattern on the seat seam must be symmetrical. If the trousers have flapped or patch pockets, these can be matched to their surrounding areas, or in the case of checks the designer has the option of cutting them on the bias. Irrespective of the matching requirements, the fabric pattern on pockets and other visible components should always be symmetrical.

Where matching and symmetry are necessary, it must be accepted that materials usage will be greater than that for garments made in plain fabrics. This increase is slight for stripes but considerable for checked fabrics. However, if for any one season checks are the fashion then the designer has, more than ever, to punctiliously examine every intended design for patterned fabrics in terms of labour and material costs.

## TO SUM UP

At first sight sample cutting might seem a relatively simple operation, but this hides the fact that the operation contains a great deal of responsibility. Apart from cutting a sample accurately and according to the characteristics of the cloth, the sample cutter also has most of the responsibility for determining the cost of the largest component in the costing of a garment – raw materials.

# 6

# *The Principles of Fusing Technology*

## INTRODUCTION

Every clothing manufacturer continually attempts to produce garments with immediate sales appeal. However, one of the most important materials used for nearly every item of outerwear has no sales appeal, because it is invisible to the consumer. This material is the fusible interlining, and since these materials were first introduced in the early 1950s, they have become an integral component of garment construction.

The term fusible interlining is used to describe a base fabric coated on one side with a thermoplastic adhesive resin which can be bonded to another fabric by the controlled application of heat and pressure. These materials, generally called fusibles, provide the designer with a number of properties which can enhance the appearance of finished garments by the following:

- Control and stabilisation of critical areas
- Reinforcement of specific design features
- Minimum of modification to the 'handle' of the top cloth
- Preservation of a crisp and fresh look.

Correctly selected and applied, fusibles have many advantages for the designer, the production unit and the consumer.

## CONSTRUCTION OF FUSIBLES

A fusible combines the following three factors in its construction:

(1) *Base material* Also called the substrate

(2) *Thermoplastic resins* Synthetic resins which melt when subjected to heat and revert to their original solid state when cooled
(3) *Coating* The amount of resin deposited and how it is secured on to the base fabric.

Fig. 6.1A shows the basic construction of a fusible and Fig. 6.1B illustrates how the resin is disbursed into the top cloth when the two layers are bonded. The finished bond is referred to as a laminate.

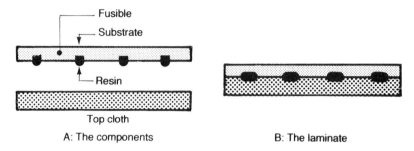

**Fig. 6.1.** Fusing.

## BASE MATERIALS

The base materials are produced in a diversity of woven, knitted and nonwoven forms, with each type having its own particular application according to its intended function on the garment. The materials can be produced from natural or synthetic fibres or from blends of each of these fibres. Base cloths influence the following characteristics of the finished garment:

- Handle and bulk
- Shape retention
- Shrinkage control
- Crease recovery
- Appearance after washing or dry cleaning
- Durability.

The properties of different base materials sometimes overlap to a considerable extent so the following descriptions contain some generalisations.

### Woven substrates
Due to their construction, woven substrates are not easily distorted by wear or cleaning and they exert a large degree of control on shrinkage and shape retention; but these properties are not particularly conducive to a soft and natural handle, which is a much sought after attribute for contemporary garments. Developments of twill weaves with fine warp

threads and thicker weft threads have improved the handle and bulk properties of this type of base cloth.

### Knitted substrates

Knitted substrates provide a degree of elasticity to the laminate by yielding, together with the top cloth, to body and limb movements. The first knitted substrates were warp knitted (Fig. 6.2A), and when weft inserted yarns were introduced into the construction (Fig. 6.2B), knitted base cloths became widely accepted for fusing to woven top cloths. A big advantage of a weft-insert substrate is that it has a natural handle whilst being resilient in the warp direction, i.e. around the body area where it is used. As the knitting process is generally faster than weaving, these materials are cheaper than woven substrates.

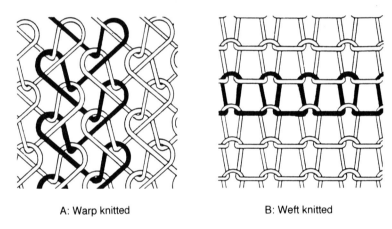

A: Warp knitted          B: Weft knitted

**Fig. 6.2.** Knitted substrates.

### Nonwoven substrates

Nonwoven substrates are made of a series or mixture of fibres held together at bond sites. The fibres can be natural, synthetic or various combinations of the two, but due to the cost of natural fibres, most nonwovens are constructed from synthetic fibres. The most commonly used fibres for general purpose fusibles are viscose, polyester, acrylic and nylon. Nylon fibres tend to produce a relatively firm substrate and are often used when a component requires additional stiffening.

The orientation of the fibres in the substrate influences its end use. The three standard web formations are:

(1)   *Random* (Fig. 6.3A)   The fibres are orientated randomly and the resultant substrate is omnidirectional. This property helps with material utilisation but the fusible itself lacks strength and resilience in any one direction.

(2)   *Parallel* (Fig. 6.3B)   As the name implies, the fibres are orientated

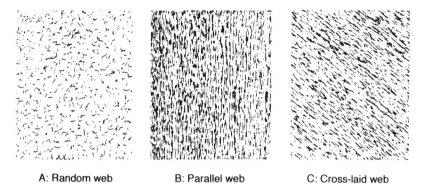

A: Random web    B: Parallel web    C: Cross-laid web

**Fig. 6.3.** Nonwoven web types.

to the length of substrate which makes this fusible ideal for preventing stretching.

(3) *Cross-laid* (Fig. 6.3C)   In this web, the fibres are orientated at an angle of 45° across the substrate, which gives the opportunity of cutting components on the true bias or on the straight.

## RESINS

Resins are the sole bonding agent between the top cloth and substrate and irrespective of the type of resin used, they have to conform to the following conditions:

- *Upper-limit temperature*   The resin should become viscous at a temperature below that which would damage the top cloth. Whilst this temperature varies according to the composition of the top cloth, it rarely exceeds 175°C.
- *Lower-limit temperature*   This is the lowest temperature at which the resin starts to become viscous. For most fusibles this is about 110°C, and for the fusibles used for leather and suede materials, the temperature is considerably lower.
- *Cleanability*   The adhesive properties of the resin have to be sufficiently strong to withstand washing and/or dry-cleaning throughout the normal life of the garment.
- *Handle*   The resin must contribute to the required handle and not act as an unwanted stiffening agent on the final laminate.

## Resin types and applications
The types and properties of the most widely used resins are:

- *Polyethylene*   At different densities this is suitable for wash and wear garments or for those which have to be dry-cleaned only.
- *Polyamide*   All polyamide resins produce full dry-cleanable and

washable bonds but there is a class of this resin which is dry-cleanable only.

- *Polyester* These resins have the same general properties as polyamides but are generally a little cheaper.
- *PVC* Used extensively for siliconised rainwear fabrics.
- *Plasticised cellulose acetate* A multi-purpose resin which is both washable and dry-cleanable.
- *Plasticised polyvinyl acetate* Mainly used for leather and fur materials but is not dry-cleanable and has very limited washability.

The general characteristics of these resins are summed up in Table 6.1.

**Table 6.1.** Resins – general characteristics.

| Resin type | Fusing system | | Durability | | Relative cost |
|---|---|---|---|---|---|
| | Steam | Electric | Wash | Dry clean | |
| Polyethylene (Low density) | Limited | Good | Suitable | Limited | Low |
| Polyethylene (High density) | Not recommended | Good | Good | Good | Medium |
| Polyamides | Good | Good | Limited | Good | High |
| Polyester | Good | Good | Limited | Good | Medium |
| Plasticised C.A. | Good | Good | Suitable | Suitable | Medium |
| Phenolics | Limited | Good | Limited | Suitable | Medium |

## COATING

There are two aspects of the coating: density and coating system.

### Density

Resins are applied to substrates in three different densities – low, medium and high – and the degree of density refers to the actual mass per unit volume of the resin material. This physical density is directly related to the melting point of the resin and its resistance to dry-cleaning solvents, and as a rule the higher the density, the better the resin stands up to dry-cleaning.

### Coating system

This refers to the process whereby the resin is deposited and secured on the substrate. There are three principal methods:

(1) *Scatter coating* This method uses electronically controlled scattering heads to deposit the resin crystals on to the moving substrate. The drawback of this method is that the substrate surface is covered with resin, which reduces the flexibility of the laminate.

(2) *Dry dot printing*   In this process the resin is printed on to the substrate in regularly spaced dots by means of rollers with indentations which hold the resin crystals. This method is generally regarded as producing the most flexible bond

(3) *Preformed*   The resin is heat processed to form a net which is then bonded onto the substrate by heat and pressure. During heating the link lines of the net melt, leaving a minute dot pattern on the base cloth. This method is also used to produce paper-backed tapes which are used for fastening hems and facings instead of blind-stitching or felling.

## FUSING PROCESS

Regardless of which fusible and machine are used, fusing is controlled by four processing components – temperature, time, pressure and cooling – and these have to be accurately combined in order to achieve the optimum results.

### Temperature
There is a limited range of temperatures that are effective for each type of resin. Too high a temperature causes the resin to become too viscous, which could result in the resin being forced through to the right side of the cloth. If the temperature is too low, the resin is not sufficiently viscous to disburse into the top cloth. In general, resin-melt temperatures range from 130°–160°C and the best results will normally occur within ±7°C of the temperature specified by the manufacturer of the fusible.

### Time
The only time element of any value during the fusing process is when the top cloth and fusible are under pressure in the heating zone of the machine. This time cycle for a particular fusible is determined by:

- Whether the fusible has a high- or low-melt resin
- If a light or heavy substrate is being used
- The nature of the top cloth being used, i.e. thick or thin, dense or open.

Manufacturers of fusibles supply data sheets which give the time cycle for each fusible, and this refers to the actual fusing stage only.

### Pressure
When the resin is viscous, pressure is applied to the top cloth and fusible assembly to ensure that:

- Full contact is made between the top cloth and fusible
- Heat transfer is at the optimum level
- There is an even penetration of the viscous resin into the fibres of the top cloth.

Most fusing machines use two steel rollers or pressure plates to create pressure, but a flexible pressure system has been developed which automatically adapts itself to variations in the thickness of the assembly being fused, whilst maintaining an even pressure over the entire assembly.

### Cooling
Enforced cooling is used so that the fused assemblies can be handled immediately after fusing. Cooling can be induced by various systems, including water-cooled plates, compressed air circulation and vacuum. Rapidly cooling the fused assemblies to 30°–35°C makes for a higher level of productivity than if operators have to wait for the assemblies to cool naturally.

### To sum up
The fusing process produces what is, in effect, the foundation of a garment and the best results can only be achieved when there is accurate and continual control of the four processing components.

### FUSING MACHINERY

A press is used for fusing and three basic types are:

(1)   Steam press
(2)   Flat bed press
(3)   Conveyor belt press.

Each type of machine has its own range of capabilities.

### Steam press
Regular steam pressing machines are not designed for fusing although some fusibles are produced for use on these machines. Pressing machines have some serious limitations regarding fusing, including:

● Inability to reach the heat levels required by the majority of resins
● The shape and size of the bucks restrict the size of the components which can be fused
● Most utility machines are not fitted with programme controls, which means that the entire process is operator controlled
● If the resin was originally activated by steam heat, the same thing can happen when garments are pressed during their production. This situation can cause serious problems with the stability of the laminates.

Regular steam pressing machines are not the ideal medium for fusing.

### Flat bed press
Flat bed presses are purpose-built fusing machines produced in a large

variety of sizes and with many types of work aids. This type of press has padded top and bottom bucks with electric heating elements in one or both bucks. The bottom buck is static and the top buck is lowered to fuse the assembly whilst under pressure, and then raised after cooling. Most of these machines are fitted with timers and programme controls and can achieve high levels of fusing quality.

### Conveyor belt press

Conveyor belt presses are also called continuous machines because they can be operated without stopping for the loading and unloading of the assemblies. The conveyor belt transports the assemblies through all the processes and the belt speed is adjustable according to the time cycle required. This type of machine is available in different lengths and widths and can be fitted with automatic feeding and unloading systems. A feature of the more modern machines is a microprocessor which can be programmed to control every element of the machine's operation.

The compact machine shown in Fig. 6.4 is designed to fuse the small quantities which are produced in the sample room. It has exactly the same range of fusing characteristics as its industrial big brother and can be fitted with a return feed system and stacker if its production has to be increased. A feature of the machine illustrated is that one side is open so as to allow for the partial fusing of wider components, such as coat foreparts.

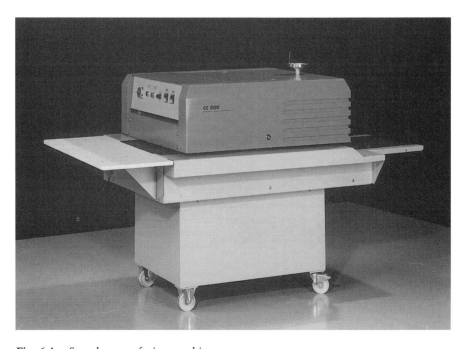

**Fig. 6.4.** Sample room fusing machine.

## THE SELECTION OF FUSIBLES

While the selection of fusibles involves some subjective factors, it does not preclude the use of a systematic and objective selection procedure which covers the following factors.

### Top cloth
It should never be assumed that fusing is possible for every cloth without checking the following points:

- Will the fusing process produce excessive shrinkage, glazing or permanent colour change?
- Does the top cloth have a siliconised finish which would adversely affect fusing quality?
- Some fabrics constructed from continuous filament yarns can be problematic as regards fusing. Trials are advisable.
- Does the top cloth have an open construction that will show the resin on the right side?
- Is there a raised pattern on the top cloth which could be damaged by the pressure used during the fusing process?

Apart from the above points, it is always worth checking the handle and draping qualities of the cloth after fusing.

### Base cloths
Different parts of the same garment could require the use of different fusibles, so the evaluation of suitability should take into account the function of the fusible in relation to the area and/or component to be fused. Nonwoven fusibles are generally cheaper than other types so these should be considered for small area reinforcements such as pockets, vent edges, hems and under collars. It is advisable to use woven or knitted substrates for large areas such as fronts, and the marker waste from these materials can be utilised for small parts.

### Resins
This concerns whether the garment will be dry-cleaned or washed, or both. The method used to clean a garment is generally determined by the properties of the top cloth, and the resin used has to match these properties.

### Cost
Cost is very important, but it should not necessarily be the sole criterion for selecting a fusible because price itself means very little unless compared to performance. The designer should always verify whether a particular fusible will enhance or degrade the design objectives of the garment.

Remember that an all-purpose fusible which suits every type of fabric and can be fused without any control over temperature, time and pressure has yet to be invented.

## PATTERNS FOR FUSIBLES

The trade terms used to describe the two main categories of outerwear body garments are 'constructed' and 'unconstructed'. Constructed garments are those which have a large number of fused areas plus a body and sleeve lining, whilst unconstructed garments have very small applications of fusibles and are generally unlined. The principles of preparing fusible component patterns for constructed or unconstructed garments are exactly the same because the final results basically required from the large or small scale use of fusibles are identical.

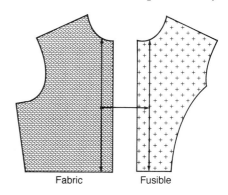

**Fig. 6.5.** The relationship between grain lines.

### Grain lines

Unless there are compelling reasons to do otherwise, the grain lines of knitted or woven fusibles should be the same as the cloth component for which the fusible is intended (Fig. 6.5). For nonwoven fusibles, the grain lines very much depend on the fibre orientation of the material being used and the function of the piece to be cut. If the nonwoven fusible has a definite fibre lay, the resultant grain line can be utilised to advantage when necessary. When the fusible is omnidirectional and has to be used, then needs must, etc.

### Seams

With the exception of armholes, shoulder seams, collar and front edges, together with edges of flaps etc, the fusible should be cut back from all seams which have to be pressed open (Fig. 6.6). The amount of the cut-back is the

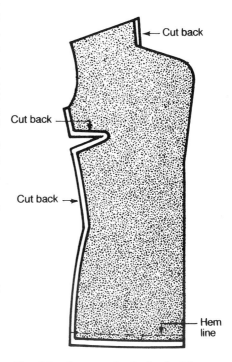

**Fig. 6.6.** Seam cut-backs for fusibles.

width of the seam allowance plus 1 or 2 mm. This reduces the final thickness of the seam and slightly lessens the degree of accuracy required by the operator when positioning the fusible on the cloth.

### Folded edges

When folds have to be made on fused cloth components, it is advantageous to extend the fusible for about 1.5 cm past the fold line (Fig. 6.7). When folded, this extension prevents stretching and helps to maintain a straight fold line.

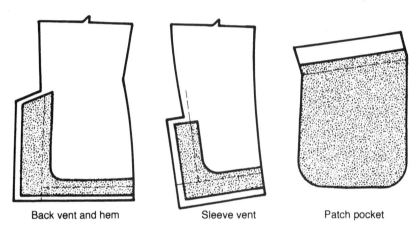

| | | |
|---|---|---|
| Back vent and hem | Sleeve vent | Patch pocket |

**Fig. 6.7.** Overlap of fusible on fold lines.

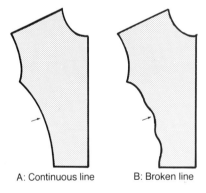

A: Continuous line      B: Broken line

**Fig. 6.8.** Breaking the edge of a fusible.

### Line breaking

On fronts that are not fully fused, the impression of the edge of the fusible can often be seen on the right side of the front. In most cases this can be eliminated by cutting the offending edge in a wave pattern instead of an unbroken line (Fig. 6.8). This procedure can also be used on other components if the same problem occurs.

### Reinforcements

These are used for a variety of applications and their main purpose is to prevent the stretching of body and sleeve hems, inset pockets, trouser flies, side pockets, etc (Fig. 6.9). Nonwoven fusibles are generally used for this purpose although it is also possible to utilise the waste areas of markers for woven and knitted fusibles if the grain lines can be observed. Another point to consider is whether to cut reinforcement components in one size only because this is a simple and labour-saving method of working.

## TO SUM UP

In comparison with most other textile materials, fusibles are precision products and the optimum results will only be achieved when they are precisely selected, cut and applied.

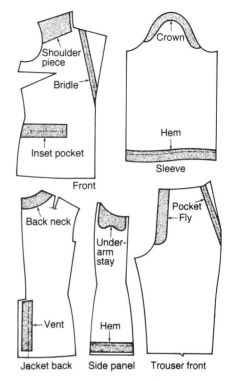

**Fig. 6.9.** Examples of fusible reinforcements.

# 7

# *The Principles of Sewing Technology*

## INTRODUCTION

Although ultrasonic welding and resin bonding systems have been developed as alternative forms, sewing still remains the most predominant method of assembling garments of all types. In every sector of the clothing industry, sewing operations are performed by a great variety of machines, each of which has the capability for specific operations on a particular category of garments and/or fabric. This wide choice of sewing machinery is also matched by those for sewing threads, needles and other auxiliary components.

In practice the word sewing covers a large number of subjects and it is only when there is a correct balance between all of them that the optimum results can be achieved. This chapter will examine the principles involved.

## THE COMPONENTS OF SEWING

Irrespective of type, all sewing machines function in a similar way and the best example for illustrating these elements is the regular sewing machine. There are five basic components of sewing (Fig. 7.1): needle, throat plate, presser foot, feed dogs and threads.

## NEEDLES

Needles have been used for hand sewing since about 18000 BC and were originally made from ivory, bone, wood and horn (Fig. 7.2). Their form has remained unchanged since then. During the fifteenth century iron needles were introduced for hand sewing, and in 1800 Balthasar Krems of Germany was the first to use a needle with the eye near the point for a

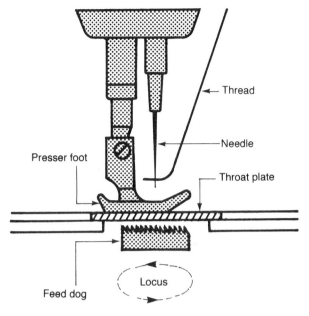

**Fig. 7.1.** The components of sewing.

chain-stitch machine he had developed. The large scale production of sewing machines started about 1840 and this was paralleled by numerous developments in the manufacture and quality of machine needles. Today the steel needle in common use is a precision product which is critical to the formation of stitches.

The functions of the sewing machine needle are to form a passage in the material through which the needle thread can wholly or partially pass and form a loop which can be picked up by the looper or hook mechanisms. Needles are made in straight or curved forms and their main construction features are (Fig. 7.3):

- *Butt* The truncated conical shape at the top of the needle which facilitates its insertion into the needle bar or clamp.
- *Shank* Usually larger in diameter than the rest of the needle, the shank can be cylindrical in shape or flat on one side, depending on the method used to secure the needle in or on the needle bar.
- *Shoulder* The section joining the shank to the blade.

**Fig. 7.2.** Wooden needle, circa 17500 BC.

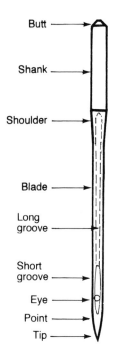

Butt

Shank

Shoulder

Blade

Long
groove

Short
groove

Eye

Point

Tip

**Fig. 7.3.**   Needle
parts.

- *Blade*   The longest section of the needle, this runs from the shoulder to the eye.
- *Grooves*   On one side of the needle there is a long groove which protects the needle thread as it enters and is withdrawn from the fabric. There is a short groove on the opposite side which extends a short distance above and below the eye and its purpose is to aid the passage of the thread into the material and loop formation.
- *Eye*   An elliptical hole between the two grooves; the shape and finish of the inside top of the eye are important factors in the prevention of thread damage during sewing.
- *Point*   This is shaped to provide the best penetration of the material being sewn.
- *Tip*   The tip, when combined with the point, determines the ease and extent of penetration into the fabric.

Points and tips have a decisive bearing on the performance of the needle and the various types of combinations can be divided into two groups:

(1)   *Round points*   These are used for the sewing of textile materials and whilst they all have a circular cross section, they differ in their tip shapes. In general, set point needles are used for most woven fabrics and the ball point needle is preferred for delicate and knitted materials. Both these points are available with light, medium or heavy tips (Fig. 7.4) and these combinations allow for good compatibility between the fabric and the needle.

(2)   *Cutting points*   These needles actually cut a hole through the material and because of this are mainly used for the sewing of leather, artificial leather and plastic materials. The points come in a variety of shapes (Fig. 7.5). They all influence the set (angle) of the stitches and as a result the appearance of a row of stitches. The individual stitches are slightly slanted instead of being in a straight line.

## SIZES

There are about twenty systems of designating needle size but the one used most widely is the metric system (Nm). This is based on the diameter of the blade multiplied by 100. For example, a needle with a blade diameter of 0.9 mm would be size Nm 90. Although needle lengths for each type of machine are standardised, longer needles are sometimes used to increase the clearance between the end of the needle bar and the work being sewn.

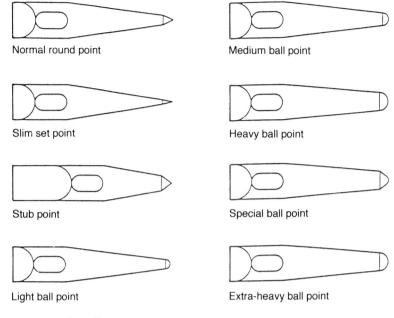

Normal round point

Medium ball point

Slim set point

Heavy ball point

Stub point

Special ball point

Light ball point

Extra-heavy ball point

**Fig. 7.4.** Round needle points.

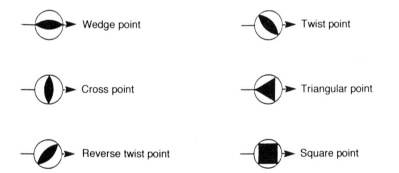

Wedge point

Twist point

Cross point

Triangular point

Reverse twist point

Square point

**Fig. 7.5.** Needle cutting points.

Some modern sewing machines can reach a speed of 15 000 rpm and a stitch is formed with every revolution. At these speeds, plus the immense range of different materials which have to be sewn, the selection of the correct needle is crucial.

## THROAT PLATE (FIG. 7.6)

The throat plate is a static component which has slots for the feed dogs, and one or more holes for needles or a slot

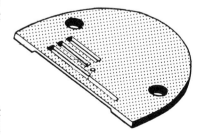

**Fig. 7.6.** Throat plate.

Fig. 7.7.   Presser foot.

for swing-needle machines such as a zigzag. The upper surface of the throat plate is highly polished so as to enable the material to slide over this area as smoothly as possible.

## PRESSER FOOT (FIG. 7.7)

The presser foot is attached to the pressure bar of the machine and its two prime purposes are to:

(1)   Hold the material securely against the throatplate and prevent it shifting during the movement of the needle.
(2)   Maintain a slight pressure contact between the material and the feed dogs to ensure that material moves at the same rate and direction as the feed dogs themselves.

Apart from the standard presser foot, there are special purpose feet which help the operator perform operations other than regular seaming. Amongst others, there are feet for piping edges, zip setting, cording, tape-binding, hemming, and those which incorporate guides for top stitching.

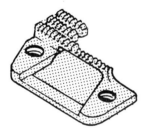

Fig. 7.8.   Feed dogs.

## FEED DOGS (FIG. 7.8)

The basic function of the feed dogs is to move the fabric forward by a distance equal to the stitch length, between successive penetrations of the needle. The feed dog itself can have one or more raised rows of serrated teeth which rise through the slots in the throat plate and slightly enmesh with the underside of the fabric. Feed dogs have an elliptical locus (movement) and this advances the material the necessary distance; the feed dogs then drop below the surface of the throatplate and are positioned ready for the next cycle. There are many types of feed dogs and feed systems and the principal ones are examined later in this chapter.

## SEWING THREADS (FIG. 7.9)

Almost all garments produced have one component in common: the sewing thread. Whilst sewing threads are usually a relatively small percentage of the cost of a garment, they have an extremely significant

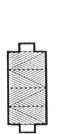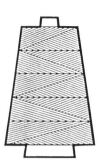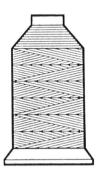

**Fig. 7.9.** Sewing threads.

influence on the appearance and durability of the finished product. The production of sewing threads is an extensive and complex subject, and the reader is well referred to *The Technology of Thread and Seams* published by Coats Ltd for a detailed coverage of the processes involved.

In practical terms, any examination of sewing threads must start with the question, What are the essential requirements for a sewing thread? The answers can be grouped under two headings, sewability and durability.

## SEWABILITY

This describes the basic all-round properties of the thread, including:

- Not breaking when used for high-speed sewing.
- Facilitating the consistent formation of stitches.
- The minimum occurrence of skipped stitches.
- In order to prevent changes in tension during sewing, the thread must have a uniform diameter.
- A high level of resistance to abrasion is essential due to the friction of the thread in the needle eye and with other mechanisms.
- The thread has to have sufficient surface smoothness to pass easily through the guides on the machine. This ensures the uniformity of stitch formation.

## DURABILITY

The main thread related factors under this heading are:

- The thread has to have sufficient elasticity to withstand the normal pressures imposed on seams during wear. This is particularly important for knitted fabrics because of their inherent extensibility.
- Thread shrinkage should be minimal after the garment has been washed or dry-cleaned. Seam puckering is often caused by unstable thread.

- It is important that the thread maintains its original colour after being subjected to cleaning processes. In particular, this applies to the threads used for top stitching and other decorative purposes such as embroidery.

## THREAD TYPES

Ideally a sewing thread should combine the best properties of sewability and durability, and whilst there are many threads available which approach this, certain compromises have to be accepted due to various technical limitations. However, for practical purposes sewing threads for the clothing industry can be divided into three broad groups: cotton, synthetics and corespun.

### Cotton

Threads made from cotton fibres have excellent sewability because the fibres are very supple and are not seriously affected by the heat generated by needles during sewing. On the other hand, cotton threads are not highly durable and some of the softer types have a tendency to shrink when the garment is washed. Glace and mercerised cotton threads sew well and have a lustrous appearance, but they both shrink slightly when wetted.

### Synthetics

This is a large group of threads made mainly from nylon, polyester rayon and polyamide filaments or fibres. The threads are very durable and are not affected by moisture or the chemicals used in washing powders or dry cleaning solvents. In addition, they have excellent dimensional stability and a high level of resistance to abrasion. Synthetic threads are available in a number of different constructions and finishes, which enhances their performance for special sewing applications.

### Corespun (Fig. 7.10)

This thread has a continuous filament polyester core wrapped in cotton fibres, which produces a strong thread with excellent sewability. Core-

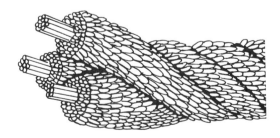

**Fig. 7.10.**   Corespun thread.

spun threads have good elasticity and a high resistance to heat and shrinkage, but cost more than regular threads because they have to be dyed twice, first for the polyester core and then for the cotton wrap. An advantage of corespun threads is that finer threads can be used due to the superior strength of the polyester core. According to Carr and Latham (1994), corespun threads represent about 50% of British sewing thread sales.

### Other fibres

Two other natural fibre threads which have limited applications are silk and linen.

- *Silk*   These threads are strong, with good elongation and a highly lustrous appearance. Silk threads have good sewability but the high cost restricts their use for mass production sewing.
- *Linen*   Once widely used for sewing tents, shoes, leather etc, threads spun from flax have been mostly replaced by synthetics.

A summary of the main characteristics of various types of threads is given in Table 7.1 but selection also has to take into account the fabric and its finish, needle size, stitch type, seam construction and the sewing speed.

### THREAD SIZES

There are many systems for defining thread size but the most widely used is the Tex number system. This is based on the gram weight of 1000 m of yarn, so a fine thread would have a low Tex number and a thick thread would have a high number. Thread manufacturers using other systems will normally provide the Tex equivalent values.

### COSTS

Price is not necessarily the sole criterion for purchasing sewing threads because it is performance which really counts. Trouble-free sewing combined with durability is essential to prevent constant work stoppages caused by continual breaks, and to avoid consumer dissatisfaction with seams that open during normal wear conditions.

## TO SUM UP

Effective sewing can only be achieved when there is an accurately balanced combination of all the components involved. It is said that the real strength of a chain is that of its weakest link, and this also applies to sewing.

**Table 7.1.** The general properties of sewing threads.

| Property / Type | Sewability | Durability | Strength | Suppleness | Abrasion resistance | Heat resistance | Colour fastness | Shrinkage resistance | Elasticity |
|---|---|---|---|---|---|---|---|---|---|
| Cotton | High | Moderate | Moderate | High | Moderate | Good | High | Moderate | Good |
| Soft cotton | High | Moderate | Moderate | Good | Moderate | Good | Good | Low | Good |
| Glace cotton | High | Moderate | Moderate | Good | Good | Good | Good | Moderate | Good |
| Mercerised cotton | High | Moderate | High | Good | High | Moderate | Good | High | Good |
| Polyester | Moderate | High | High | Good | High | Moderate | Good | High | Good |
| Polyamide (nylon) | Moderate | High | High | Good | High | Good | Good | High | Moderate |
| Polyester cotton | High | High | High | High | Good | Good | Moderate | High | Good |

## FEED SYSTEMS

Feed systems relate to the combination of the needle, throat plate, presser foot and feed dogs which control the feed of the material from stitch to stitch whilst regulating the relationship between the plies being sewn. Some examples are given here.

### Drop feed (Fig. 7.11A)
This is the standard feed system for regular sewing machines where there is little or no likelihood that the ply alignment will be distorted during sewing.

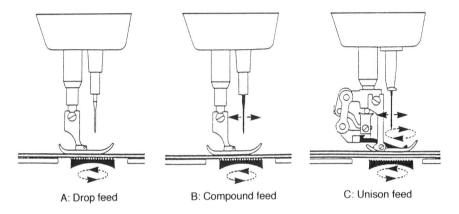

| A: Drop feed | B: Compound feed | C: Unison feed |

**Fig. 7.11.** Examples of feed systems.

### Compound feed (7.11B)
With this feed system, the needle and feed dog movements are synchronised to ensure that the plies retain their correct alignment during sewing. This system is used for sewing slippery materials such as velvet and also for edge stitching.

### Unison feed (Fig. 7.11C)
This system is also known as a 'walking foot' system because the presser foot has two independently driven sections: the holding and the feeding feet (Fig. 7.12). These two sections alternately advance and hold the plies in alignment, an important requirement when sewing bulky seams in heavy weight materials.

### Differential feed (Fig. 7.13)
These systems have two independently operated feed dogs, one behind and one in front of the needle. The feed dogs can be regulated so as to create fullness on the upper or lower ply of the seam; for example, easing the back shoulder seam onto the front shoulder seam.

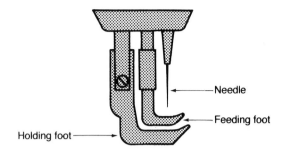

**Fig. 7.12.** Unison feed – walking feet.

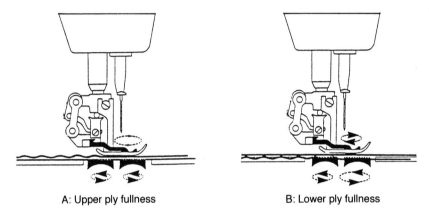

A: Upper ply fullness                              B: Lower ply fullness

**Fig. 7.13.** Differential feed system.

There are also a number of mechanisms which are used as auxiliary feed systems where there are special feed requirements, such as embroidery machines and automatic long-seamers used for closing the leg seams of trousers.

## STITCHES AND SEAMS

Stitches and seams are the basic elements of sewing, and national and international standards have been developed for accurately classifying them. Some examples are given here.

## STITCHES

The basic classes in British Standard 3870 Part 1 are:

*Class 100*   These are chain stitches formed from a needle thread only and they are typically used for basting, felling and blindstitching.

*Class 200* Originally hand stitches, these are mostly formed by single threads passed from one side of the material to the other with each successive penetration of the needle. Various classes of this stitch are used for saddle stitching and the prick stitching of edges.

*Class 300* These are also referred to as lock stitches because the top and under groups of threads are interlaced to form the stitch. The most widely used stitch formation in this class is no. 301 (Fig. 7.14), which is that produced by a regular sewing machine.

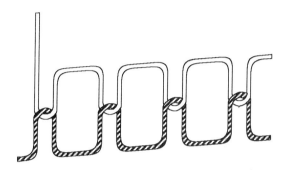

**Fig. 7.14.** Stitch type 301: two-thread lock stitch.

*Class 400* Formed by two or more groups of threads, the loops of which are interlaced and interlooped, stitch no. 401 (Fig. 7.15) is a chain stitch formed from two threads and is widely used for knitted materials because the stitch formation makes for good extensibility and lateral strength.

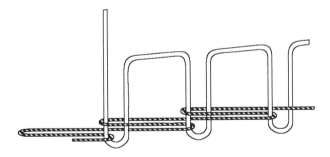

**Fig. 7.15.** Stitch type 401: two-thread chain stitch.

*Class 500* These are known as overedge stitches because at least one group of threads covers the edge of the material. In this class, stitch no. 504 is a three-thread overlocking stitch used for assembling light weight knits and also for cleaning and finishing the seam and hem edges of garments.

When the 401 chain stitch and the 504 overlock stitch are sewn simultaneously they form what is called a five-thread safety stitch where the chain and overlock stitches are not connected This stitch combination is widely used for seaming denim and cheaper grades of trousers. Another class of safety stitch, sometimes called a mock safety stitch, is formed from four threads where one or two of the overlock threads interlace with the needle thread. This stitch class is used for assembling garments made from light weight materials and sometimes for linings. Due to their construction, safety stitched seams cannot be pressed open but have to be pressed to one side which, with heavy weight materials, is apt to create a bulky seam appearance.

*Class 600:* There are many complex stitch formations in this class because the stitches can be formed from three to nine threads and the use of up to four needles. This class of stitches is characterised by high elasticity and strength and is frequently used for flat butted seams (Fig. 7.16) in the corsetry and underwear sectors of the clothing industry.

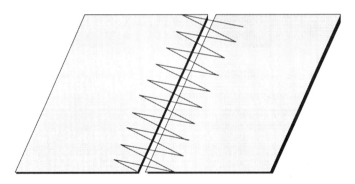

**Fig. 7.16.** Flat butted seam.

*Class 700:* This is a single thread lock stitch similar to the 300 class, which has very limited applications because of its inherent weakness.

*Class 800:* This class covers combinations of two or more stitch classes which are sewn simultaneously, like the five thread safety stitch. Different versions of this class are used for the assembly of swimwear.

## SEAMS

British Standard 3870:1991 classifies seam constructions under eight headings. Typical examples are given here and shown in Fig. 7.17.

*Class 1 – superimposed* This seam is constructed with a minimum of two components and is the most widely used seam construction in this class. Among others, safety stitched and French seams are covered by this class.

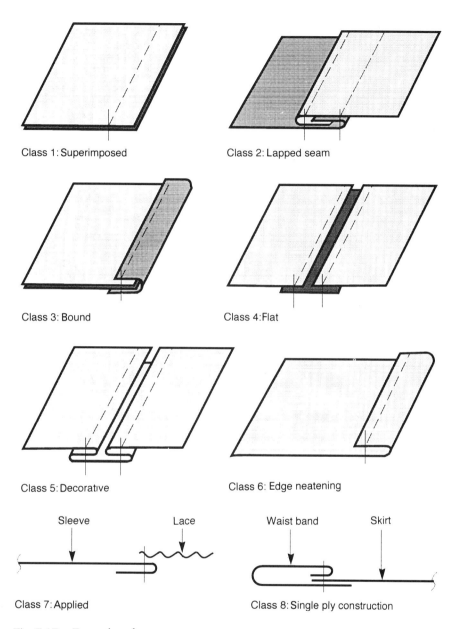

Class 1: Superimposed

Class 2: Lapped seam

Class 3: Bound

Class 4: Flat

Class 5: Decorative

Class 6: Edge neatening

Sleeve    Lace

Class 7: Applied

Waist band    Skirt

Class 8: Single ply construction

**Fig. 7.17.** Examples of seam types.

*Class 2 – lapped*   The best example of this class is the lapped seam construction used for many denim articles and for certain types of blouses and shirts.

*Class 3 – bound*   Used for constructing a decorative edge binding from self or other material such as tape.

*Class 4 – flat*   In this class the seam edges do not overlap but are butted together.

*Class 5 – decorative*   This construction consists of a row or rows of stitches sewn through one or more plies of fabric. The channel seam shown in Fig. 7.17 is representative of this class.

*Class 6 – edge neatening*   This could refer to the overlocked edge of a single ply or to the single turned overlocked hem of a blouse.

*Class 7*   These are sometimes called applied seams because they are mainly used to apply a decorative material to an edge or seam, such as the lace edging on a nightdress sleeve.

*Class 8*   Constructed from one ply of fabric only, this class is commonly used for belts and belt loops. Fig. 7.17 illustrates one version of this class whereby the waist band is simultaneously folded and stitched onto the waist line of a skirt.

Standard classifications for stitches and seams are indispensable because apart from reducing ambiguity in communication, the definitions enable a more precise focus to be made when considering these two fundamental elements of sewing.

# MACHINERY AND EQUIPMENT

## INTRODUCTION

Since the mid 1980s many technological advances have been made to the sewing machinery which is used for the production of clothing. New construction materials and improved electronic systems have played an important role in these advances. They include:

- *'Dry-Machines'*   These machines are manufactured with sealed anti-friction bearings, which eliminates oil changes during the normal working life of the machine.
- *Variable speed electronic motors*   Machines such as bartackers and automatic seamers have to sew over considerably different thicknesses of materials and seam constructions. Where the machine had one sewing speed only, snapped threads and broken needles were a frequent occurrence when sewing over varying thicknesses. It is now possible to adjust the machine's sewing speed according to what has to be sewn, and this capability makes a positive contribution to the improvement of productivity.
- *Integrated motor*   Instead of the drive motor being mounted sepa-

rately under the table, it is now integrated with the machine head as one unit.

## USER FRIENDLY

Sewing machine manufacturers are now seriously taking into account the operators who will use their machines and are incorporating many of the following items into their designs:

- Machines now have large clearances in their main working areas, which facilitates the easy and comfortable manipulation of work during sewing. The positions and shapes of a machine's control elements are ergonomically designed so as to suit the natural movement range and convenience of the operator.
- In accordance with new safety regulations, machines have built-in safety devices which protect the operator and the machine against operational errors.
- Specially designed stands are available for machines where the operator works in a standing instead of a seated position. The standing working position is a distinctive feature of quick-response types of production systems.
- Machines are painted in colours that are easy on the eye and which fit in with the dynamic colour schemes used in modern factories.

These are just a few of the innovations which, with many others, are gradually becoming standard features for all types of sewing machines.

## BASIC MACHINES

A comprehensive review of all the different machines on the market is beyond the scope of this book, but the following are some of the machines most widely used for the production of clothing.

### Regular sewing machine (Fig. 7.18)
This machine is the basic workhorse of the clothing industry and has numerous applications due to the great variety of work aids and feed systems available for it. Some of the main features of this class of machine are:

- They are generally available in three versions for sewing light, medium or heavy weight materials.
- With the addition of a programmable microprocessor control system, the machine can be programmed for repetitive operations such as sewing around labels or stitching simple decorative elements.
- Many versions of this machine have bobbins which hold 50% more thread than the conventional bobbin. An electronic monitoring

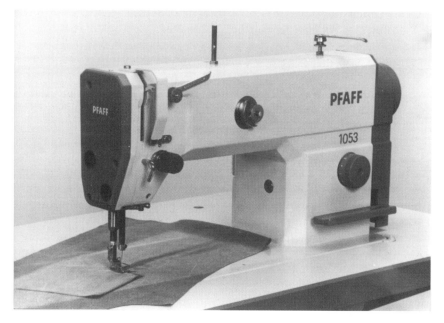

**Fig. 7.18.** High speed regular sewing machine.

system ensures that when the bobbin is changed, no seam interruption is visible on the top part of the side being sewn.
* Electronically controlled thread cutting, tacking, needle positioning and foot lifting systems have become standard equipment on these and many other machines.

### Lockstitch bartacker (Fig. 7.19)
This class of machine has a wide range of applications apart from regular bartacking operations. It can easily be converted to sew an endless variety of stitch patterns in an area 6 cm × 6 cm where the pattern contains up to 72 stitches. Sewing speed is adjustable according to the thickness of the part being sewn, and the free cylinder arm makes handling easier when bartacking on cylindrical sections of garments such as belt loops, pocket corners and trouser flies.

### Lockstitch buttonhole machine (Fig. 7.20)
The machine illustrated is for sewing buttonholes in light weight materials, such as those used for blouses, dresses and shirts. In one continuous operation the machine sews a rectangular shaped buttonhole by means of purl-stitch, and both ends are secured by a bartack. The machine is operated by one pedal only and the head can be mounted in the length or across the width of the work top, depending on whether vertical or horizontal buttonholes are being sewn.

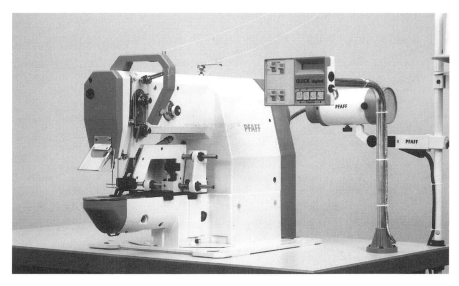

**Fig. 7.19.** Lockstitch bartacker.

**Fig. 7.20.** Lockstitch buttonhole machine.

## Three-thread overlock with a microprocessor (Fig. 7.21)

Based on a regular overlock machine, this version is used for the assembly seaming of garments made up in light weight knitted materials. The microprocessor enables the accurate calibration of stitch tension without manually adjusting the spring tensioners, and permits automatic

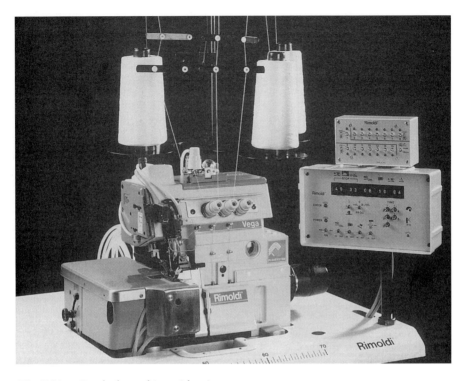

**Fig. 7.21.** Overlock machine with microprocessor.

cutting of the thread chain at the beginning and end of seams. A 'tractor-foot' can be fitted to this machine when sewing seams with varying thicknesses.

## Blind stitch machine
These machines are available in different versions for blind stitching the hems and facings of garments made in materials ranging from sheer to heavy weight. The machine forms a single-thread stitch and can sew up to 3000 stitches per minute. Stitch penetration control is digitally displayed and most machines are fitted with thread trimmers and a stitch condensing device which prevents the end of the sewing from unravelling. Fig. 7.22 shows a hem sewn by this type of machine.

## Single-thread button sewing machine (Fig. 7.23)
The machine shown has an electronically controlled system which automatically feeds correctly positioned buttons directly from the button hopper on the right into the button clamp. It is easily adjusted for sewing two or four hole buttons, and changing the number of stitches, say from 10 to 20, just requires pressing a knob on the front of the machine. A special version of this machine has a needle penetration control whereby just two of the total stitches sewn are visible on the facing whilst the others are sewn through the forepart and fusible only.

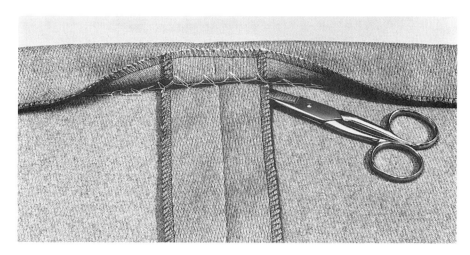

**Fig. 7.22.** Blind stitched hem.

**Fig. 7.23.** Button sewing machine with automatic button feed.

## TO SUM UP

With all the versatility of highly skilled machine operators, there is no real substitute for the right machine for the job.

# 8

# The Principles of Pressing Technology

## INTRODUCTION

Pressing can be defined as a process which changes the geometric fibre structure of the area being pressed by the controlled application of heat, steam and pressure. In this sense, removing a crease from a garment involves the same change of fibre lay as that required to open a seam or to press a hem.

With very few exceptions, every type of product manufactured by the clothing industry is pressed either during and at the end of its assembly or at the end only. The exceptions are items of corsetry and underwear which, due to the materials and construction, do not require any form of pressing. At the other extreme from these 'non-pressed' garments, the pressing operations required for a man's constructed jacket can account for about 25% of the total production time for the jacket. Regardless of the extent of pressing which garments undergo, pressing is a crucial process which imparts the final finish to a garment. A garment always has greater hanger or package appeal if it is fresh looking and crisply pressed.

## CLASSIFICATIONS OF PRESSING

The total process of pressing can be divided into two groups of operations: under pressing and top pressing.

### UNDER PRESSING

This term covers all of the operations performed on garments during their assembly. Seam opening, dart pressing and the pressing of flaps and patches are typical operations within this group.

Under pressing, when broken down into a sequence of operations, not only makes successive operations a little easier, but also enhances garment quality. For example, it is far easier for an operator to press a panelled back well if the component is on its own rather than closed to the shoulders and side seams of the fronts. This example demonstrates a good working principle for under pressing: when possible, the component should be positioned naturally during pressing and should not be constricted by other parts.

## TOP PRESSING

Sometimes referred to as off-pressing, this group includes all the operations used to finish garments when they have been completely assembled. The operations involved can range from a simple smoothing-out with a hand iron to about fifteen machine and hand operations which are required to top press a woman's lined coat. The extent of the operations is determined by the construction of the garment, the fabric and, in some cases, how well the garment has been under pressed during its production.

There is no doubt that top pressing is the major process for finishing a garment and giving it its final appearance, but top pressing can only achieve the best results when performed on well made-up garments. Top pressing a faultily produced garment might help to ameliorate some of the faults, but it will never make a good garment out of what is basically a bad garment.

## THE COMPONENTS OF PRESSING

Regardless of fabric, type of garment or the machinery and equipment employed, the majority of pressing operations have the same components (Fig. 8.1).

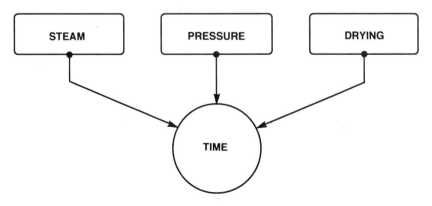

**Fig. 8.1.** The components of pressing.

## STEAM

The purpose of using pressurised steam is to relax the fibre structure of the fabric and make it pliable enough to be moulded by manipulation and pressure. Steam itself is an odourless, invisible gas consisting of vapourised water, and its white cloudy appearance is caused by minute water droplets interspersed in the vapour.

In factories, steam is generated by boilers fired by electricity or fossil fuels such as coal, gas or oil. Depending on the number of pressing work stations in the factory, steam can be distributed from a central boiler room or by small boilers located close to the work station. There are also independent pressing units which have a built-in boiler for generating their own steam.

Steam is a flexible, adaptable and efficient component of pressing. Some of its outstanding features are:

- It has a very high heat content
- Its heat is generated at a constant temperature
- It can be easily distributed and controlled
- Water is relatively cheap and plentiful.

Steam has been used throughout the centuries for pressing and it is still the best medium for this purpose.

## PRESSURE

After steaming, manual or mechanical pressure is used to change the geometric fibre lay of the area being pressed. A simple example of this change is the pressing open of a regular seam. Figure 8.2A shows the fibre geometry of the cloth after the seam has been sewn and all the fibres are laying in one plane. After softening the fibre formation by steam and the application of pressure, each side of the seam has been folded back through 180° to lay flat on the component (Fig. 8.2B). This structural change is typical of the majority of pressing operations.

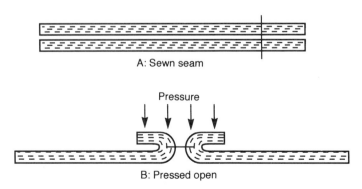

Fig. 8.2. Change of fibre lay through pressure.

## DRYING

Following the applications of steam and pressure, the area which has undergone these processes has to be dried and cooled in order that the fabric can revert to its natural moisture content and stable condition. The drying process is usually performed by a central vacuum pump which is connected to the pressing units, or by pumps built into the machine itself. The vacuum action removes the residual moisture from the material while it is laying on the pressing area.

## TIME

The length of time to which a component or garment is subjected to steaming, pressure and drying is a combined function of steam temperature, garment construction and the physical properties of the fabric being pressed. Whilst there are no fixed rules for the duration of these components, experience is a good teacher.

Accurate control of the four components of pressing is essential to the maintenance of uniform quality. This is one of the main reasons why modern pressing machines can be programmed for the duration, operating conditions and sequence of all of the elements within a specific pressing operation.

# MACHINERY AND EQUIPMENT

The first mechanically operated pressing machine was introduced in 1905, and for the next 70 years or so many advances were made in constructing specialised machines and improving their methods of operation. Despite that, the pressing department remained the technological orphan of clothing factories and it is only since the early 1980s that pressing has become a high-tech operation. For many years pressing machines were built around the traditional tailoring methods of pressing, but with the advent of synthetic materials, fusibles and more scientific pattern making systems, pressing gradually became 'engineered' rather than an imprecise copy of manual operations. The major lines of development are described here.

## PROGRAMMING

To reduce the reliance on skilled operators, various mechanical and electrical programming devices were developed which enabled the sequence and duration of the elements within an operation to be planned in advance. These systems required the operator simply to position the garment correctly on the machine with the aid of spotlight projectors which aligned with selected seams, and then to actuate the programme. In the 1990s microprocessors came into wider use and these enable the programming of operations for the pressing of different types of materials. The memory of the microprocessor holds these programs and the operator selects the one appropriate to the material to be pressed. This approach is very much in line with the developments in sewing machinery which reduce the skill input required from the operator and thus ensure the standard performance of an operation, together with consistent quality.

## COMBINATIONS

Handling was always a large element in the time involved during and between pressing operations; when the 'one machine, one operation' approach was dominant, the garment had to be handled constantly. Today the trend is to combine a series of contiguous operations into one machine thus eliminating the handling between the different operations performed by the machine. For example, the top pressing of the shoulder, sleeve head and armhole once required three separate machines. These three operations have been combined into one machine, with a significant reduction of handling time. Whilst individual specialised machines are still needed, the continuing development of combination machines has a high priority for the manufacturers of pressing machinery.

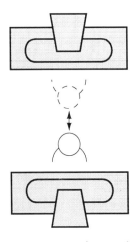

**Fig. 8.3.** Tandem work station.

## WAITING TIME

Conventionally the operator loaded the programmed machine, actuated the program, waited until it was finished and then unloaded the machine. Obviously the operator's waiting time was nonproductive time. The first attempt to reduce this wasteful factor was by arranging what are called tandem work stations (Fig. 8.3). This consisted of two machines positioned opposite each other, with the machines able to perform the same or consecutive operations. The idea was that instead of the operator waiting for the completion of an operation, the machines would be operated alternately thus reducing waiting time.

This approach gradually led to the development of carousel machines which, in principle, operated as shown with this example relating to the under or top pressing of the left and right foreparts of a coat or jacket (Fig. 8.4):

- The circular plate of the machine holds two pairs of the lower bucks with a pair of top bucks supported on the back frame.
- The operator loads one pair of fronts on the free lower bucks and then

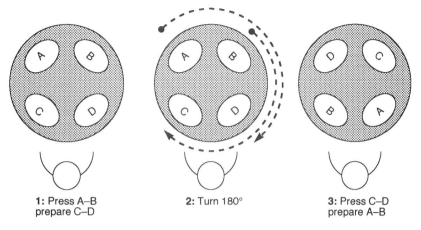

**1: Press A–B**
prepare C–D

**2: Turn 180°**

**3: Press C–D**
prepare A–B

**Fig. 8.4.** Action of 180° carousel.

actuates the circular plate. This action turns the loaded bucks through
180° to the back of the machine and simultaneously brings the pair of
bucks from the back to face the operator.

• Whilst the pair of fronts are being pressed at the back of the machine,
the operator is able to unload the returned bucks and reload them
ready for the next cycle.

Carousel type machines have two other advantages over conventional
pressing machines:

(1) As all the pressing is carried out at the back of the machine, the
operator is not continually working in a hot and steamy atmo-
sphere.

(2) The vertical action of the top bucks provides more accurate alignment and pressure distribution between the top and bottom bucks
than with the action of a regular scissor action machine (Fig. 8.5).

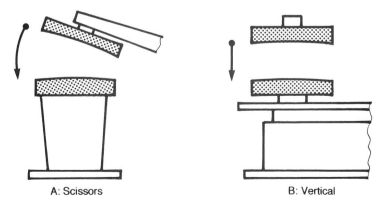

A: Scissors

B: Vertical

**Fig. 8.5.** Top buck actions.

The use of carousel machines for many under and top pressing operations is now established in most clothing factories.

## FLEXIBILITY

Not so long ago most under pressing operations were performed on a flat table, with or without the help of a sleeve board. The operator had to press every shape and form with these primitive tools and this required a great deal of skill in order to prevent the possible distortion of components. In addition, very few of these work stations had vacuum actions which meant that the operator had to let the hand iron dwell on the work in order to dry it.

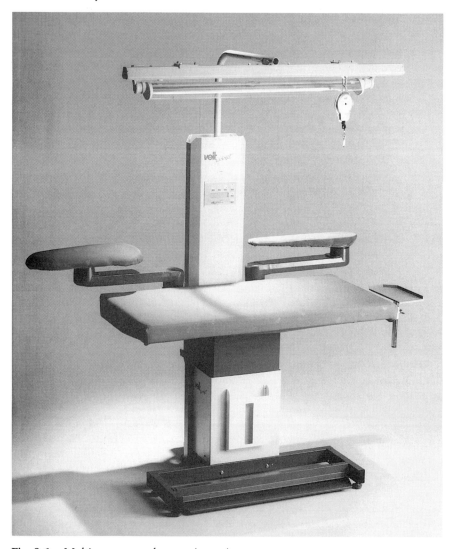

**Fig. 8.6.** Multi-purpose under pressing unit.

Modern under pressing units (Fig. 8.6) are now fitted with two or three swivel arms, each of which supports a small buck that is designed for a specific purpose. The majority of these work stations have a vacuum action connected to the table and the bucks, and some have a warm compressed air system which generates a slight air cushion between the pressing area and the component. This air cushion prevents direct contact between the buck and the work, thus reducing the possibility of shine on the pressed area.

Today the pressing department of a modern clothing factory has a technological level equal to that of most of the other production departments. The application of high-tech systems to pressing makes possible the optimum combination of quality and quantity.

## TYPES OF MACHINERY AND EQUIPMENT

Sample rooms are rarely equipped with all the machinery and equipment required to completely press sample garments. It is possible to press samples of light clothing, such as dresses, blouses and nightdresses, on a versatile unit equipped with a hand iron. However, if the samples are of constructed garments, while most of the simple under pressing operations can be performed with a hand iron, there are still several operations which require the specialised machines in the factory. This is especially relevant to top pressing where most of the operations are performed on special purpose machines. The usual procedure is for the sample room to do what can be done correctly and then use the factory's machines for everything else.

There are hundreds of different types of pressing machines on the market because of the variety of garment types produced, each with its own specific pressing requirements. The rest of this section will examine some of the items which are representative of their type.

### Hand irons

Figure 8.7 shows a typical electric high-pressure steam iron which is used for numerous operations in the production of clothing. The iron illustrated weighs 1.5 kg and the separate temperature control has an accuracy of ±2°C.

Hand irons are produced in a variety of shapes and weights to suit specific types of operation.

Figure 8.8 shows some examples of the sole plate shapes available.

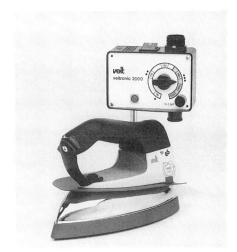

Fig. 8.7.  Electric steam iron.

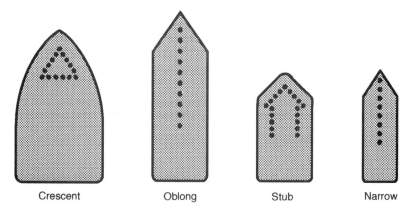

Crescent      Oblong      Stub      Narrow

**Fig. 8.8.** Sole plate shapes.

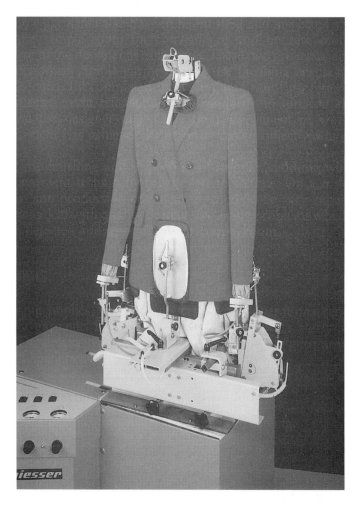

**Fig. 8.9.** Form finishing machine.

The form finishing machine in Fig. 8.9 is one of the types used for finishing men's and women's jackets, blousons and skirts. During the pressing operation the body and sleeves are precisely tensioned by pneumatically operated clamps or pressure pads which can be set for individual forms. A microprocessor monitors and regulates the programmed times, temperatures and the sequence or combination of steam, hot air, cold air and vacuum.

The small cabinet press shown in Fig. 8.10 is designed to press and heatset shirts before they are buttoned, thus preventing button marks on the finished article. During the pressing process the back and front are tensioned by air-filled bags, which ensures an even pressing surface when the shirt is between the two shaped pressing plates. This particular machine can be efficiently operated by one person only when there is a reasonable balance between the handling and pressing cycle times.

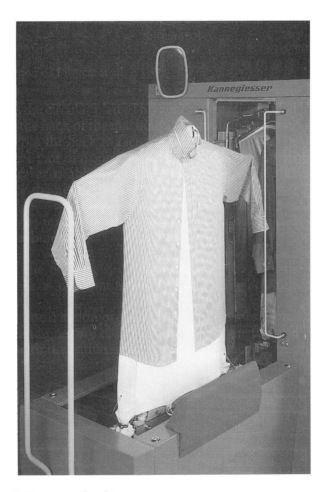

**Fig. 8.10.** Cabinet press for shirts.

**Fig. 8.11.** Tunnel finisher for knitwear.

The unit illustrated in Fig. 8.11 is a tunnel finisher for knitwear which can carry up to 30 articles at a time through the finishing processes. The tunnel has two sections, one for gentle steaming and the other for quick drying of the garment. Garment forms can be adjusted for different styling and sizes and the microprocessor controls the processing time, steaming time and the quantity and steam and air temperatures. Up to 24 individual pressing programs can be stored in the microprocessor.

A high-tech pressing machine for men's and women's clothing is illustrated in Fig. 8.12. This machine has a digital programmer and presses the shoulder, sleeve head and sleeve cuff in one set-up.

## TO SUM UP

It is no exaggeration to say that apart from cutting, the two cornerstones of garment quality are fusing and pressing. Fusing creates the foundation of the garment and the pressing processes give the final finish and appearance. The importance of pressing should never be underestimated, because of its decisive contribution to garment quality and appeal.

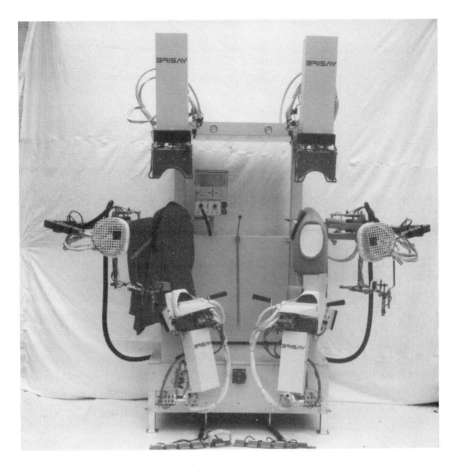

**Fig. 8.12.** High-tech pressing machine.

# 9
# Garment Finishing and Inspection

Finishing and inspection are the last two major operations in the manufacture of garments before they are bagged or boxed and delivered to the finished goods warehouse. In most factories these two operations are performed by separate departments.

All sample garments also have to be finished and inspected and this is done in the sample room for convenience and because of the close involvement of the designer at each stage. These two processes are vital in the production of sample garments because finishing ensures that the garment is correctly completed in every detail, and inspection verifies that it conforms to the relevant quality standards. In addition, this is the stage when the designer makes the final assessment of whether the sample garment has achieved its planned design objectives and can be approved.

During the finishing and inspection of samples, nothing which concerns the garment technically can be left to chance. Once orders have been taken and production commenced, it could be very expensive for the factory to deal with quality or manufacturing problems which should have been detected and rectified in the sample room.

## FINISHING

As the name implies, finishing covers all the operations required to complete a garment. For most garments this process starts after top pressing. The details involved in finishing vary according to garment type but in principle are as described here.

### ATTACHING BUTTONS

Attaching buttons has two stages, marking and sewing.

## Marking

The hand marking of button positions requires accuracy in four respects:

(1) For symmetrical garments the button positions have to ensure the overall symmetry of the garment. Some of the important points to observe are:

- Collar ends and lapel steps on both fronts must be the same distance down from the neck line
- Pockets have to be at the same height
- Lateral seams need to be matched across the fronts
- Darts should start and finish at the same levels.

(2) The button spacings have to be exact in order to ensure flat laying fronts
(3) The specified wrap allowance must be observed
(4) With striped or checked materials, pattern symmetry and alignment are essential.

## Sewing

The buttons of classic shirt and blouse samples are generally sewn on during production by automatic button sewers. These machines can be set for specific spacings and the buttons are automatically fed to the button clamp. As factories producing these types of garments mostly work to standard spacings, sewing the buttons on to the occasional sample does not interfere too much with production.

The buttoning of garments when they have been completed is usually performed in the sample room as this is more convenient than using the button sewing machines in the factory. Buttons should not be sewn onto garments which will be subjected to pressure during their top pressing. Apart from leaving an impression of the button on the cloth, there is also every possibility that the button could be broken by the pressure of the pressing machine bucks. Knitted and other garments which are steam finished only can be safely buttoned before top pressing.

## LABELS

Labels are of great benefit for the wearer, and an important aspect of finishing sample garments is to ensure that the correct labels are in the right positions. Some labels are attached during the production of the sample, whilst others are sewn on when the garment is being finished. Most companies have a standard specification for the types and positions of labels on their garments.

There are legal requirements for some types of garment labels, such as:

- Flammability of materials used for children's nightwear
- Fibre content, for example 35% cotton–65% polyester

- Garments produced for export have to carry a 'country of origin' label. This is usually inserted on the brand label.

Although there are no legal directives at the time of writing concerning the following labels, most clothing manufacturers use them to provide guidance for the consumer:

- *Care labels* These provide very specific information regarding washing and ironing temperatures, whether or not bleaching agents can be used, and the suitable types of dry cleaning solvents etc.
- *Size labels* These have to be suitable to the country or countries where the garment is to be sold. It is pointless to export garments carrying British or EEC sizing system labels to a country using a totally different sizing nomenclature. Whenever possible, the size labels should be positioned so as to be immediately visible and not necessitate a search on the part of the prospective purchaser.

Irrespective of the number and types of labels used for a garment, they should:

- Be of an acceptable size
- Maintain their legibility after repeated washing or dry cleaning during the normal life of the garment
- Be securely affixed to the garment. It does not do much for the quality image of a garment if labels flap around loosely or fall off after a short period of wear.
- Be easily seen by the consumer and not hidden away in awkward places.

In factories labels are attached by a variety of machines, ranging from the regular sewing machine to microprocessor controlled machines which hold the memories required to attach different sized labels. Some of these machines also have an automatic label feed and positioning system which only requires the operator to position the component or garment correctly.

## CLEANING

The last stage of the finishing process is to thoroughly clean the garment of all thread ends and stains. This means that the sample has to be gone over very carefully because nothing gives a worse impression to a buyer than trailing threads or unremoved stains on the inside or outside of the garment.

## FINAL TOUCHES

Sample garments often require some hand finishing with steam. A very effective tool for this is the stand-mounted iron shown in Fig. 9.1. The height and angle of the iron can be adjusted in order to operate it in a static position, or it can be removed and used by hand. A steam brush can be fitted to the iron sole when it is used to remove shine and marks from velours, velvet and other napped cloths.

When the sample garment has been checked for finish it is ready for the final phase of its manufacture – inspection – before it leaves the sample room.

## INSPECTION

Inspection is crucial for sample garments because apart from design considerations, there are a number of important factors involved. This is the moment

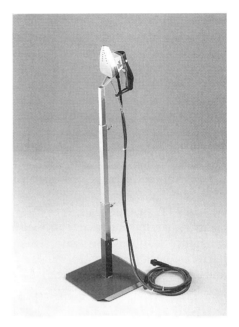

**Fig. 9.1.** Stand-mounted finishing iron.

when the sample receives the go or no-go signal and this decision requires some practical considerations on the part of the designer. The principal factors involved are given here.

### FITTING QUALITY

There are two basic approaches to fitting quality. The one used may be company policy or may be based more on custom and usage, and this dictates how the sample room has to work. The two approaches are live models and workroom stands:

### Live models
Many companies produce samples to fit the men, women or children who will model garments for buyers. This means that the sample room has to produce two patterns for each garment, one for the model and one for production. Although the differences between the two patterns could be slight, models do not have the same build and measurements as the average person and this is an added complication to the sampling procedure. Obviously there are benefits to be gained from the live models approach but making and trying-out two samples is an expensive business.

### Workroom stands
Modern workroom stands are constructed according to the results of scientific anthropometric surveys and they embody an accurate combi-

nation of the figuration and measurements of a specific population group. In effect the workroom stand mirrors the targeted potential consumer who generally has different physical characteristics from those of a professional model. For practical and commercial purposes, the workroom stand is the principal criterion for measurements and basic fitting.

There seems to be an obvious answer to the dilemma of live models or workroom stands. Why not use models having the same or very similar measurements to those of the stands used for samples? Unfortunately this is difficult to achieve because the nature of their profession demands that models should have a close resemblance to the concept of an ideal form. This concept is more than somewhat divorced from the realities of commercial sizing.

There is a practical solution to the problem of judging the fitting quality of samples. Sample garments should be made from production patterns for the workroom stand and then checked for ease of movement and fitting quality on the model. This approach does not rule out the possibility of some minor alteration to the sample in order to enhance its appearance on the model. This is of particular significance because changing the measurements and fitting of a model-based pattern to a production pattern can lead to a host of new technical problems which no one really needs.

## MEASUREMENTS

An integral part of the inspection of samples is the checking of finished measurements. Whilst measurements do not fully indicate fitting quality, checking is necessary especially if the garment has to conform to a customer's measurement specification.

The checking of garment measurements has to take into account the question of reasonable tolerances which do not have a noticeable influence on the fitting, design and functionality of the garment. Tolerances can be defined as the allowable deviations from standards, and in practical terms this requires a sense of proportion. The deviation of 0.5 cm in the length of a dress which should be 100 cm long is not the same as a deviation of 0.5 cm in the length of a shoulder having an intended length of 12.5 cm. Therefore every deviation should be considered in relation to the planned length or size of the part being measured.

## VIEWING THE GARMENT

The most effective method of viewing a sample garment to inspect its detailed and general appearance is to look at it in the same way as the consumer does in a shop, but with a professional eye. This means that the shop situation should be duplicated in the sample room and requires a very simple arrangement.

A full length cheval mirror should be positioned close to a convenient wall, with a workroom stand facing it at a distance of 1.20 m to 1.50 m. The inspector needs to stand behind the stand, look over its shoulder and view the garment in the mirror (Fig. 9.2). The recommended routine is to view the garment in four consecutive stages, revolving the stand through 90° after completing each stage. Start with the front view, follow with the first side view, then the back, and finish with the second side. When viewing, the eyes should move in a tight zigzag pattern from side to side, starting at the neckline and gradually working down to the hem. Good lighting is essential and by using this method very little will escape the eye of an alert inspector.

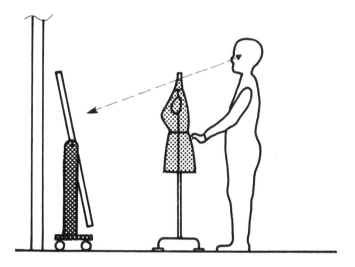

**Fig. 9.2.** Sample inspection station.

In addition to inspecting the external appearance of a sample, it is no less important to inspect the internal appearance. This inspection is necessary for all types of garments because sewing faults or other errors are easily seen on unlined garments, and stains or damages are very noticeable on linings. Today consumers have increasing demands for garment quality, and inspecting the internal and external appearance of a garment is an integral part of the quality chain which fundamentally starts in the sample room.

## QUALITY STANDARDS

The inspection of a sample garment has to be relevant to its price and target market. There is no practical reason to apply stringent quality standards to samples which, if mass produced, will only undergo the most rudimentary of inspection procedures. It is often said that a thing should be done only as well as it needs to be done, and this is very true of clothing. There is no one universal quality standard for all garments, but rather each category of garment has its own quality criteria. After all, there is a significant difference between the acceptable quality of a garment bought off a stall in a street market and that of a garment purchased from a reputable store.

However, both these retail outlets purchase merchandise from clothing manufacturers and every manufacturer attempts to cater, as best as possible, for a specific market sector. Clothing producers of all types require buyers and it is the bottom line of the balance sheet which counts in business and not necessarily citations for quality.

## WORKING METHODS

This section could also be entitled 'the follow-up' because in most factories sampling does not end with the production of sample garments. Checking samples has far broader implications.

Some factories employ the 'sealed-sample' system whereby a sample garment is given the seal of approval and marked accordingly. It is then used by the production unit as the standard for quality and production. There are some operations, such as top pressing, which are difficult to define in a garment quality specification and it is far more practical and effective to use a garment to demonstrate what is required, rather than to rely on words. In this instance one picture really is worth a thousand words.

A widely used method of checking the quality and production viability of a sample is to produce a pilot-run under factory conditions. Usually the number of garments in a pilot-run is that which can be cut from one roll of cloth, but each company has its own ideas of what is necessary as regards quantity. Pilot-run garments are closely followed-up during their production and the feedback to the designer and pattern cutter is almost immediate. Some of the larger retail organisations request grading trials in order to check the sizing of the garments on order, and often the grading trials are used by the factory as pilot-runs.

One thing is certain: garment quality should never be left to chance and the combination of exacting inspection procedures for samples and the feedback from pilot-runs goes a long way towards eliminating any chance elements.

## TO SUM UP

A great deal of responsibility is involved when a completed sample is handed over to the marketing department. By this action the designer has confirmed that the garment meets all the planned, relevant commercial and technical criteria, and above all that the quality is precisely what is required.

# 10

# The Sample Room

## INTRODUCTION

In factories, production units work on bulk and according to pre-planned production processes and inspection routines. Production operators specialise in relatively small operations, with nearly every operation performed on a machine or item of equipment constructed expressly for the purpose. The work flow is balanced and, all things being equal, these factory units operate with a consistent rhythm. In its own way the sample room also manufactures clothing but its production is strongly characterised by the intermittent nature of its working. Every new sample garment presents a new combination of design and technical problems and solutions have to be found whilst the garment is in production.

Whilst sample production contains a large number of standard operations, new operations are continually being developed and sometimes these necessitate a considerable amount of trial and error work. New types of fabrics are frequently being tried out and their reactions to fusing, sewing and pressing have to be closely observed and modifications made when called for. Fashion designers and pattern cutters are not omnipotent and often changes are made during a sample garment's production. These changes nearly always require new or adjusted patterns and possibly the revision of the original materials usage quantities. In addition, the designer could ask to see a sample garment at various stages in order to check if certain ideas are working, whether a new fabric is proving to be suitable, etc.

Producing samples is a sporadic operation which requires close and active direction by management in order to achieve the planned objectives.

## OPERATIONAL CONDITIONS

Unlike a regular production unit which works within a uniform structure, the sample room operates under different conditions for the following reasons:

- In the majority of sample rooms the standard unit of production is a single garment. Some companies also produce in the sample room the copy samples required for agents and representatives, although this is rather a misuse of highly-skilled labour.
- Every new sample garment is unique by virtue of its design and/or fabric. As a sample it is a one-off garment which is only brought to life in the sample room and when completed and approved, it is handed over to the marketing department.
- The sample room is not generally equipped with all the same types of specialised machines as those in the factory. Consequently, when necessary, some operations required for samples have to be performed outside the sample room. At times this means that sample garments have to wait until a production operator is free to carry out the work. This is yet another small factor which contributes to the intermittent nature of sample room production.
- As the sample room staff have to produce constantly changing products, their versatility, adaptability and quality is, in most cases, more important than their speed. They are not specialists in the same sense as production operators because they are specialists in making samples and not in performing a few short operations at a high rate. Therefore, whilst time is an important factor regarding sample production, it has to be on a far looser scale than the time standards used by the factory.

The operating conditions of the sample room are in sharp contrast to those prevailing in the factory, although both units are concerned with producing garments. Hence it follows that there must also be a considerable difference between their production methods.

## PRODUCTION METHODS

If anything is the key to the production methods used in the sample room it is the scale of operation. The production of two or three samples daily is totally different from producing, say, 20 or 30 samples per day. This is not just a numerical difference which can be dealt with by more people, machinery and space, but it demands a completely different approach to the concept of sample production. The following two examples examine the major disparities between the small- and large-scale production of samples.

### SMALL-SCALE

In a small-scale set-up, apart from a sample cutter there might only be three or four operators. The production method most often used in this situation is called 'making-through'. As its name suggests, an individual operator performs nearly every operation required to make a sample. A typical unit could have one operator doing all the special machine operations, such as overlocking, blind-stitching and buttonholes, as well as helping out with other work when needed. The other operators would concentrate on sewing, handwork and pressing, plus whatever else was necessary to complete the garment. The layout of this type of sample room has to be convenient for the operators but no more than that, because basically only one operator controls the work flow of a garment.

This production method requires highly skilled and versatile personnel and although it is somewhat expensive, it is a practical and effective way of producing small numbers of samples.

## LARGE-SCALE

In a sample room producing a large number of samples every day, the production method would lean towards that used by a small and well-organised factory production unit. The work would be broken down into groups of related operations, with operators mainly specialising in one group only. These groups could be:

- Special machine operations
- All types of sewing
- Under pressing
- Finishing
- Top pressing
- Inspection, etc.

The layout would be planned so that garments advance progressively from group to group without the need for constant back-tracking on the part of the operators. Whilst this production method also relies to a large extent on the versatility of its personnel, the operators are able to develop specialist group skills instead of being jacks of all trades.

## FACTORY PRODUCED SAMPLES

The previous two examples of production methods include a limited reliance on the facilities of the factory to carry out operations for which the sample room lacks the necessary specialised machinery or equipment. The construction of some types of garments, such as women's corsetry, requires an extensive range of specialised machinery and it is not viable to equip the sample room with this.

In this situation the sample room would cut the sample and then a member of the staff would accompany and guide it through the factory, from process to process. When the sample had completed its tour of the factory, the sample room would then attend to the finishing and inspection details. This method of producing samples is not particularly convenient but is a practical alternative to equipping another small factory in the sample room.

# PERSONNEL AND RESPONSIBILITIES

As mentioned previously, the sample room staff have to possess the professional attributes needed for the production of samples. Every operator has a definite area of responsibility regarding their own work and that of their co-workers. Sample garments do not have ready prepared detailed specifications because specifications are derived from approved samples and not the other way round. As a result, the specification is gradually built up in the sample room and as it is practically impossible to continually watch over every operation, the personnel have to be relied upon to take full responsibility for what they are doing. What this means for different kinds of operator is explained here.

### Cutters

Initially cutters have to verify that the requisite tests on materials have been carried out, and in the event of serious deviations they need to report them and obtain approval to cut the sample. Disregarding this elementary procedure could involve the company in the bulk purchase of unsuitable materials. Irrespective of whether the cutting markers are prepared manually or on a CAD system, the cutter has to be able to evaluate accurately a marker's efficiency. He or she has to be sufficiently responsible to know when it is justified to call in the designer to examine possible pattern modifications which could improve material usage.

### Sewing machine operators

Sewing machine operators have a wide range of responsibilities including the correct selection of needles and threads, determining the appropriate stitch length, verifying seam strength and checking on possible seam damage, especially when new materials are being tried out. The sewing machine operator also has to be a good judge of a pattern's accuracy and practicality and has a responsibility to inform the pattern cutter if there are any pattern related problems.

### Special machine operators

Special machine operators have to know a great deal about many machines and be capable of making sound appraisals of the performance of each one on every fabric being worked on. Most competent special machine operators know how to adjust their various machines according to specific demands, but they also have to know when to request the assistance of a mechanic if the problem is beyond their know-how. Calling on a mechanic is more responsible behaviour than giving up and saying that the operation cannot be done.

## Pressers

The responsibilities of pressers extend to two main aspects:

(1)   When incorrect work reaches them, they should be able to recognise faults and be sufficiently familiar with the operations in the sample room to know who to inform regarding the mistakes.
(2)   Their practical evaluations of the reactions of a particular material to pressing can be critical to the decision to purchase the material.

Pressers do not only press the output of previous sewing or other operations but they are also contributing to the final appearance of the sample. They have to be aware of this responsibility and do far more than open seams or press hems.

## Finishing

This group of operations also have responsibilities because operators working on finishing can often see small details that need correction before the sample is produced in bulk. It is relatively easy to cover up most of these small details by some additional handwork or by other means, but factories cannot afford this type of extraneous work. The finishing operative who has a sense of responsibility would point out these errors to the appropriate person.

## Quality

There has to be an individual and joint responsibility on the part of the sample room staff regarding the quality of the garments which they produce. Every employee has to be fully acquainted with the required quality standards and be capable of making independent and objective judgements of the quality of their own work. They also have to help each other by pointing out quality errors to their co-workers. This is not a point-scoring situation but rather an honest acceptance of the collective responsibility for sample quality. Another worker may not be perfect, but then neither are you.

## Training

Due to natural labour turnover there will always be a small group of learners in the sample room. An essential part of their initiation into work is to thoroughly acquaint them with the responsibilities which go with their particular job.

## TO SUM UP

The objective of any production system is to produce efficiently the planned number of garments within the allocated time and at the required quality. Conditions and the scale of operation have a great influence on how the sample room operates, but despite this every opportunity has to be maximised.

# PART 3

# DESIGN DEPARTMENT OPERATION

# 11

# *Communication*

The communication of information is an integral part of the day-to-day working routine in the design department. In operational terms, these communications have three forms:

(1) The garment identification system used within the company
(2) The means and the type of information by which the designer communicates with the design and sample room staff at the inception of the design.
(3) The form and content of the information which has to be communicated to other departments on the completion and handing over of the sample garment.

In all instances the accuracy of the information transmitted is important because there is no place for guesswork in an organisation which wants to be efficient.

## GARMENT IDENTIFICATION

Nearly every person working for a clothing manufacturer is dealing with garments in one way or another, and communication between them is simplified if they all use the same terminology to define the products they are handling. One method of achieving a simple common language is to use working style numbers as the basic code of communication. An example of this follows.

### EXAMPLE

It is preferable to use a four figure working style number rather than a computer generated number which can run into seven or eight alpha-

| X | O | O | O |  | O | X | O | O |  | O | O | X | X |
|---|---|---|---|---|---|---|---|---|---|---|---|---|---|

| Garment | N° | Season | Phase | N° | Consecutive number per garment category |
|---|---|---|---|---|---|
| Skirts | 1 | Spring | 1 | 1 | |
| Trousers | 2 | Spring | 2 | 2 | 01 |
| Dresses | 3 | Summer | 1 | 3 | |
| Blouses | 4 | Autumn | 1 | 4 | |
| Vests | 5 | Winter | 1 | 5 | |
| Jackets | 6 | Winter | 2 | 6 | 99 |

A: Numbering method

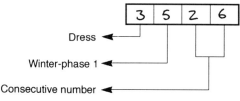

Dress ◄───
Winter-phase 1 ◄───
Consecutive number ◄───

B: Working style number

**Fig. 11.1.** Principles of style numbering system.

numeric characters that are not easy to remember. Figure 11.1A shows an example of a unique style numbering system. The significance of each of the four numbers is:

### First number
This denotes the garment category, i.e.

1 = Skirts      2 = Trousers      3 = Dresses etc

Therefore the type of garment being dealt with is immediately recognisable by its first number.

### Second number
Seasons are usually divided into phases and the seasons with their individual phases, recur every year. The objective of the second number is to introduce a time context for a garment so that people will know whether it belongs to the past, current or future season, and to what phase of that particular season. The central column of Fig. 11.1A shows how this aspect of the numbering system operates.

### Third and fourth numbers
These refer to the consecutive numbers given to the successive garments

developed in each garment category. The example system can accommodate 99 different garments in one category for one phase of a season.

Fig. 11.1B shows a working style number developed by this method and with a little experience of the system it should tell precisely the same information to all concerned.

## DESIGNER TO STAFF

Once the decision has been taken to develop a particular design, the design will remain only an idea unless it is translated into a garment. This means that the designer has to prepare a design specification which is a detailed and precise presentation of the planned design and technical objectives of the garment. This specification can have both formal and informal aspects because some details, such as materials, have definite references, whereas the description of a design feature can be in the shorthand language of the design department. For example, a material could have the number 4062, but a collar might be described as 'about 2 cm wider all round than style 605'. Some of the items which a design specification should contain are given here.

### Working sketch

This is sometimes called a croquis and is intended as a pure working drawing and not as a fashion journal illustration. Apart from the regular front and back views, this sketch should also show any new or complex design features drawn to a legible scale. All the appropriate design information should be written on the sketch so that the pattern cutter and other members of the staff know exactly what is involved.

### Size and measurements

Although sample garments are generally all made in the same size, there can be exceptions, so the required sample size has to be recorded. Some customers request that samples should be made according to their size charts, in which case the relevant information has to be noted on the design specification. If the sample has any features which have special measurements, these too should be noted.

### Special processes

This refers to all processes which are not within the regular framework, such as pleating, embroidery and the use of special packaging. Everything which comes under this heading should be listed and, if necessary, accompanied by a small sample or sketch.

### Fabrics

Cuttings of all the materials to be used should be attached to the specification and their complete details recorded. If there are any special comments regarding a particular material, these have to be noted.

In theory new materials should arrive at the sample room after undergoing the requisite tests, but where no formal procedures exist for testing sample lengths, the sample section has to do its own basic testing. In the main this concerns checking the reaction of top cloths to pressing and fusing. If anything more than an acceptable level of reaction occurs, the material should be carefully evaluated as to whether it can be used or needs to be rejected. Materials such as linings and fusibles from suppliers with proven track records do not have to be tested prior to cutting each new sample, but an occasional test is a wise precaution.

## Trimmings

Under this heading are details of all the other materials which have been selected for use on the sample. Among others these include buttons, press studs, pads, decorative tapes, zips, appliqués and special sewing threads.

The extent of this part of the design specification is dependent on the category of garment produced by the company. Specifying all the trimmings for a fully constructed garment is considerably more extensive than for a school blouse. But whatever the variety of trimmings required for a sample garment, nothing should be omitted.

## Labels

While this subject has been covered in the previous chapter, there are some additional points which are particularly relevant to sample garments, covering two aspects:

(1)  *Label type*  The type and format of labels used by a company is usually standardised and for the design specification it is a question of selecting and noting those which are applicable. Many labels are printed and if there are different requirements from the stock items, say for care labels, these have to be ordered. Brand labels are generally held in stock by the trimmings stores.
(2)  *Label positioning*  Most companies have standard guidelines for the positioning of labels and any planned deviations from this standard have to be noted on the design specification.

## IMPORTANCE OF THE SPECIFICATION

In a practical sense, the design specification is the primary planning and control tool for a sample garment. Without it the people involved with producing samples have no definite information as to what to do and how. Verbal instructions can be misunderstood or forgotten, so it is essential that the sample room staff have a written and illustrated specification of exactly what is required. Figure 11.2 shows an example of the design specification for a woman's outsize jacket, together with some items of information possibly needed for administration purposes.

What is fundamental to a design specification is not the amount of information it contains but the accuracy and relevance of the informa-

| DESIGN SPECIFICATION | | | | | | |
|---|---|---|---|---|---|---|
| Season/phase | Description | Number | Size | Make-up | Designer | Pattern |
| Spring/2 | Outsize Jacket | 644 | 22 | Standard | Janet | Mark. |

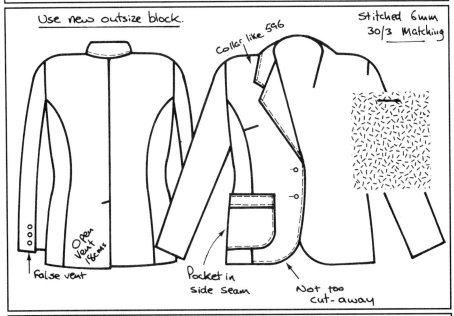

Use new outsize block.

Collar like 596

Stitched 6mm 30/3 Matching

Open Vent 16cms

False vent

Pocket in side seam

Not too cut-away

| Top cloths | | | | | Buttons | | | |
|---|---|---|---|---|---|---|---|---|
| | Supplier | Nº | Compo. | Colour | Supplier | Type | Size | Colour |
| 1 | Texall | 6164 | 100% wool | Beige 22 | Bu Honit | 465 | Body 32 | Matching |
| 2 | | | | | —"— | 465 | Sleeves 24 | —.— |
| 3 | | | | | | | | |

| Linings | | | | | Labels | | |
|---|---|---|---|---|---|---|---|
| | Supplier | Nº | Colour | For | Label | Type | Position |
| 1 | Linetex | 551 | Beige | Body sleeves | Brand/size | Gerlin | Back Neck. |
| 2 | | | | | Composition | 100% wool | Left side seam |
| | | | | | Care | Dry clean only | —.— |

| Fusibles | | | | | Pads | Supplier | Type | Size |
|---|---|---|---|---|---|---|---|---|
| | Supplier | Nº | Colour | For | | Pollster | 1361 | L |
| 1 | Fuse mat | 388 | Beige | Fronts | Special instructions | | | |
| 2 | —"— | 210 | Beige | Collar Patch. | Check cloth shrinkage | | | |
| 3 | —"— | 408 | White | Reinfor. | No spare buttons | | | |

**Fig. 11.2.**   Example of design specification.

tion which it communicates. Ideally, the specification should answer every practical question in advance.

## FROM THE DESIGN DEPARTMENT

After a sample garment has been checked and approved by the designer, it is ready to be handed over to the marketing department together with all the information required to prepare a costing. In the majority of factories, the design department is not expected to provide accurate and finalised costings for sample garments, but to collate and present a reliable basis for the costing clerk to work from.

There are a number of practical reasons why the design department is not the realistic place for garment costings, as explained below.

The preparation of garment costings requires people specialising in the subject and these people are not generally working members of the design team. Specialisation implies a specific area of expertise and both designers and costing clerks are experts in their respective fields. Therefore the most efficient results for the company are achieved when employees concentrate on what they do best and are not given extraneous tasks for which they have little working expertise.

The sample room cuts single-size markers and whilst the sample cutter will attempt to be as economical as possible, a skilled marker planner will nearly always achieve better results. If the sample room pattern has been constructed on a CAD system, it can be easily transferred to the marker planner in the factory cutting room in order to obtain accurate figures regarding materials requirements. If manual methods are used, the factory's marker planner should be called in to check over the pattern arrangements made in the sample room before figures are finalised.

Some companies, especially those producing for stock, calculate materials requirements on the basis of markers containing a fixed ratio of sizes. Again it is not practical for the sample room to become involved in this extensive and skilled work, so it is better left to the experts.

The price of materials and trimmings is often open to negotiation with suppliers, and the designer is not usually involved in this side of the business. The designer will have ordered sample materials knowing that the quoted prices are within the planned framework, but this price is not always the actual price which the company will pay.

Although sample garments are planned to be produced within a standard work-content framework, many deviations occur during their making-up. The precise analysis of work-content and operations in order to establish labour costs is the work of a skilled clothing technician, even though the sample room could possibly provide an intelligent guesstimate.

Finally, it is in the best interests of a company to have 'horses for courses' rather than a free-for-all situation.

## SAMPLE SUMMARY SHEET

The sample room accrues a great deal of pertinent information concerning each sample from start to finish, and this information has to be communicated to people responsible for analysis and costing. It should be emphasised that this information is not a costing but rather a reasonably dependable basis from which a costing can be developed. For example purposes, the medium by which the information is communicated can be called a sample summary sheet (Fig. 11.3). (The outsize jacket illustrated on the sample summary sheet in Fig. 11.3 is the end product of that shown in the design specification in Fig. 11.2.)

The objectives of this document are to provide other specialist functions in the company with a fairly accurate and comprehensive summary of what has been invested in a sample as regards materials, trimmings and labour. When the information on this sheet has been processed, it not only generates the garment costing but it also provides the basis for all the production and logistic planning concerned with a particular garment. Consequently, its compilation requires some punctilious work on the part of the design department.

The extent of the summary sheet is obviously dependent on the relative complexity of the garment category manufactured by the company, but the following are some typical examples of the items which could appear on this document:

(1)   A sketch of the sample plus, when relevant, illustrations of any new or unique design features. It is not really necessary for this sketch to have the written content of the design specification.

(2)   Each and every type of material and the quantities used for the sample have to be listed. If there have been difficulties with any particular material, this should be pointed out and the reasons stated. This is important because it might be necessary to change the material in order to prevent future problems with quality or in production processes.

(3)   Every trimming used must be listed in the same detail as the materials. Nothing should be overlooked because each item, however small, is part of the logistics chain for production. Imagine the situation if the factory had to put hundreds of uncompleted garments aside not just because a needed item of trim had not been ordered, but even worse because no one even knew that the item was needed for the garments. So on the summary sheet every small item must be considered indispensable information.

(4)   Full particulars of any outside services used, such as embroidery, must be recorded. If the provider of the service is new to the company, it helps to include the name to contact.

(5)   Attention should be drawn to any special processes employed when making up the sample. This is important for the production department as it enables them to plan in advance rather than discover new special operations at the last minute.

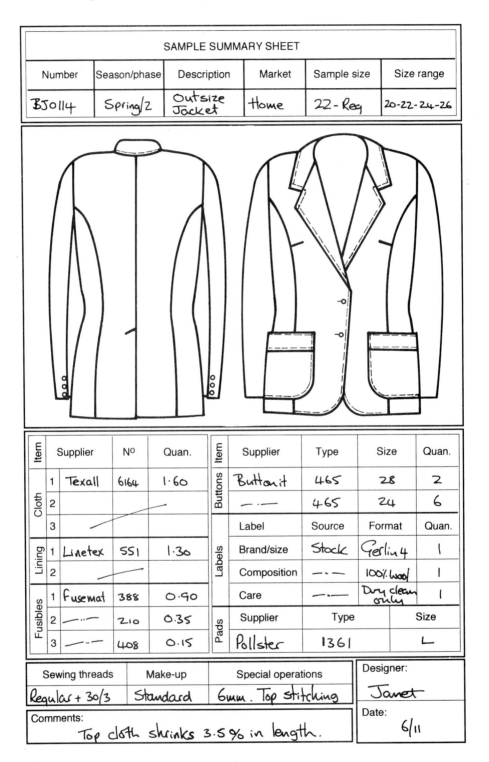

| | SAMPLE SUMMARY SHEET | | | | |
|---|---|---|---|---|---|
| Number | Season/phase | Description | Market | Sample size | Size range |
| BJ0114 | Spring/2 | Outsize Jacket | Home | 22 - Reg | 20-22-24-26 |

| Item | Supplier | Nº | Quan. | Item | Supplier | Type | Size | Quan. |
|---|---|---|---|---|---|---|---|---|
| Cloth 1 | Texall | 6164 | 1.60 | Buttons | Button it | 465 | 28 | 2 |
| Cloth 2 | | | | | —.— | 465 | 24 | 6 |
| Cloth 3 | | | | | Label | Source | Format | Quan. |
| Lining 1 | Linetex | 551 | 1.30 | Labels | Brand/size | Stock | Gerlin 4 | 1 |
| Lining 2 | | | | | Composition | —.— | 100% wool | 1 |
| Fusibles 1 | Fusemat | 388 | 0.90 | | Care | —.— | Dry clean only | 1 |
| Fusibles 2 | —..— | 210 | 0.35 | Pads | Supplier | Type | Size | |
| Fusibles 3 | —.— | 408 | 0.15 | | Pollster | 1361 | L | |

| Sewing threads | Make-up | Special operations | Designer: |
|---|---|---|---|
| Regular + 30/3 | Standard | 6mm. Top stitching | Janet |
| Comments: Top cloth shrinks 3.5% in length. | | | Date: 6/11 |

**Fig. 11.3.** Sample summary sheet.

(6)   There are also a number of company procedures to observe, mainly concerned with garment identification. From an administrative point of view, this information is no less important than any other items on the sheet.

## TO SUM UP

As buzz-words, information and communication have been around for a long time. Today everybody actively engaged in commercial and industrial activities is conscious of the operative importance of these two words. In a clothing manufacturing company, the designer plays a pivotal role in the interchange of information because all the garments produced by the company start their existence in the design department.

# 12

# *Management and Organisation*

## INTRODUCTION

Although at first glance it might seem a little odd to discuss management in a book of this nature, management is essential for all organised activity, and regardless of size the design department is no exception. The formal process whereby somebody is appointed to be in charge of the department means that for all practical purposes this person is the manager and has to operate the department with all that the word management involves. As designers are usually selected for this position, they have to understand something about the principles of management in order to contribute to the professional performance of the department.

The extent of the managerial activities involved is very much dependent on the sizes of the design and sample sections and the organisation of the working relationship between them. In a small factory where there might be only five or six people concerned with design and sample production, they could all probably work comfortably together in one large room. The designer in charge can see everything that is going on and managing the operation of a unit this size is more hands-on than through remote control. Obviously the elements of organisation, planning and control have to be used but they are relatively simple to apply.

On the other hand a large-scale manufacturer of fashion wear would operate a big design department which needs more space and personnel and a great deal of applied management skills. In a set-up of this nature, where the design department is responsible for the production of a large quantity of sample garments, the total operation would probably be divided into two groups., the design section and the sample room.

### Design section
This group works closely with the marketing department and would be responsible for all the design and design-related activities, plus the in-

process and final approval of samples. If the company produces a range of different garment types, the design section could be subdivided into design groups specialising in one type of garment. Each of these groups would comprise designers, stylists, pattern cutters, etc, and would be headed by an appropriate member of the team. The heads of these teams would receive their design briefings from the department's manager or manageress who would also give the final approval to the samples produced by each group.

### Sample room

This is where the sample garments are cut, made and finished, and in a large-scale operation this department would require very active management to ensure its effective operation. Normally this department would be managed by a person who has had extensive practical experience with the garments produced by the company and who also knows and can interpret the idiosyncrasies of each designer. The sample room supervisor would work in close co-ordination with the design room staff and would be accountable to the manager or manageress of the department.

## THE PRINCIPLES

How the design and sample sections are organised and managed is mainly a question of scale, but whatever the circumstances the same principles are applicable and these include: the following aspects.

### MANAGEMENT

Management is often described in terms of techniques, formulae and procedures. While these are pertinent to sophisticated industrial and commercial environments, the management of the design department is a far less complex situation. At this level management is a relatively simple operation which combines a social and systematic approach because decisions are implemented by people working according to the manager's evaluation of the facts.

For the design department management can be considered the systematic planning and control of activities within an organised framework, which enables the personnel to work productively and happily.

### ORGANISATION

All groups of people working together require an organisational structure in order to form them into a complete and functioning unit. Due to the nature of its work, the design department has no need for a strictly prescribed organisation; more of a 'free-wheeling' but responsible approach is appropriate. Every member of the department has to be aware of their specific operational responsibilities, how far they can go in any given situation and to whom they are accountable.

Apart from creating a known and structured working environment, good organisation also provides people with a feeling of security in the sense of belonging to a group and participating in a united effort.

## PLANNING AND CONTROL

Planning is concerned with setting realistic objectives and providing the means to achieve them, whilst control establishes the criteria and procedures needed to check the progress and results of what has been planned. For the design department the functions of planning and control are indispensable, because without them nobody knows exactly what to do, when to do it and with what to do it. If planning is non-existent, control procedures are worthless because there are no predetermined criteria for comparison.

Even the smallest design department has to plan its work in advance so that sample collections will be available for the marketing department by the right date. Time is an important factor in the production of sample garments and collection completion dates determine priorities and objectives. Therefore a small department which plans its work according to time alone is automatically provided with a rudimentary but practical method of global control.

The larger design department requires a more detailed form of planning and control due to the number of people working at different tasks on numerous sample garments. If the company has a substantial export business, planning is of paramount importance because the department has to produce collections for different seasons parallel to those being produced for their home market. A department of this size is literally a sample factory and it has to employ similar planning and control techniques to those used by a small industrial production unit.

However, there is a difference between the scales of planning and control for a factory and for a design department. In a factory these two functions are built around bulk work and the performance of groups, whereas in a design department single garments are the unit of production and most of the work is performed by individuals.

## CO-ORDINATION

The objectives of co-ordination are to ensure a balanced and suitable allocation of tasks between all the people directly involved with designing and producing sample garments. To a great extent co-ordination is based on recorded data or the accumulated experience of what people are capable of doing during a specific time. This knowledge has to be applied when planning a balanced work flow between:

- Designers and stylists
- Pattern cutters
- Sample cutters
- Sample production personnel
- Inspection personnel etc.

Approved designs are handed over to pattern cutters, each of whom might have unique areas of expertise. Consequently the allocation of designs to the pattern cutters has to take into account the general and specific capabilities and work rate of each one so that the load is spread equitably. When patterns are completed, the next stage is cutting and this requires two elements of co-ordination:

(1) That all the materials and trimmings needed for samples are on hand when they are due to be cut
(2) That the department has sufficient sample cutters to cope with the planned daily quantity.

The sewing, pressing, finishing and inspection of samples is carried out by a group of employees with a known individual and group capability. These capabilities have to be carefully balanced so that each individual can make an effective contribution to the group's overall performance.

The co-ordination of activities is central to the competent operation of the design department. Working in a stop–start situation caused by a lack of co-ordination is not particularly conducive to efficiency and motivation.

## PERSONNEL

As a group the people in the design department need to be versatile specialists because of the dynamics of the fashion business. Designers are continually developing designs in new materials, and pattern cutters have to cope with an extremely high rate of style changes. The sample room operators do not have a learning period for each new sample but have to manage with an explanation and then produce a first-time garment in the shortest possible time.

This situation demands a high level of professionalism from everyone involved, and in this context professionalism means:

(1) That the person is a fully trained and experienced expert in his or her field of specialisation
(2) That the person has a professional approach to their work and can operate independently and conscientiously without the need for constant supervision and direction.

The selection of personnel is an exacting process because, regardless of the manager's own abilities, a manager will ultimately only be as good as the people working for him.

## MOTIVATION

Apart from being a place of business, a company is also a working day social centre and managers have to possess and apply social skills in addition to their other management skills. Motivation has long been recognised as an important tool of management and without it a group of employees will never really be fused into a smoothly working team making a united effort. Obviously motivation in itself will not create high performance levels if people lack the appropriate qualifications. But if they have ability and are well trained, motivation will significantly enhance both individual and collective levels of performance.

When people are treated fairly and are well motivated, they find a form of social anchorage in their work place and this makes an important contribution to the level of their participation. This can only be created by management who set a personal example and have an active awareness of the value of motivation.

# THE PRACTICE OF MANAGEMENT

The extent of managerial activities in the design department is relative to its size, but whatever size the department does have to be managed. Some practical pointers are given below.

## RESPONSIBILITY AND AUTHORITY

When a person is appointed to manage the department, he or she is automatically made accountable for the results. This is responsibility, but this alone is insufficient for effective management if the same person is not given the equivalent scale of authority. In other words, if the manager has the full responsibility for running the department, then he or she has to be vested with the full authority to act according to the scope and terms of the responsibility.

## ADMINISTRATION

There are usually many administrative procedures which have to be dealt with in the day-to-day work of a manager. Some of these are part of the company's internal administrative systems, whilst many others are directly concerned with personnel.

Internal systems will only work well if they are continually updated with accurate information, so the manager has a clear responsibility in this direction. Where people are concerned, administrative details should be attended to correctly and promptly because dealing with people's problems is part of the human relations network within the department.

## ADVANCEMENT

Many people working in the department have professional ambitions, and often the department has similar ambitions for the same people. When the ambitions are the same on both sides, the manager has a responsibility to realise them as well as possible.

Whether it concerns a raise in salary, promotion or a transfer to another type of work, if the change is justified it should be effected at the most propitious time. An employee who has to wait an unreasonable length of time for a decision is apt to become a frustrated employee, with all the associated negative aspects. It does much for the general morale in the department if the personnel know that ability and application will be recognised and rewarded.

## TRAINING

Due to changing demands, it is not always possible to keep an employee continuously on the work to which he or she is accustomed. Consequently the manager needs to consider the possibility of training some members of staff to perform other operations. Given sufficient experience with their new operations, these people can always help out when the pressure is on, apart from being a reserve in the event of absences. The production of sample garments requires a high level of versatility and the investment in developing additional proficiencies is always worthwhile.

## PLANNING AND CONTROL

These two inseparable activities are the tools by which management sets objectives and is enabled to verify results. It is essential that all the work of the design department is planned in advance and that control systems are set up in order that the status and progress of the plans can be evaluated. Some examples are given below.

## DESIGN PROGRAMME

The example of a design programme in Fig. 12.1 is for a company producing skirts and it covers the various collections required for the first phase of the forthcoming winter season. The programme works as follows.

The allocation of collections between the designers involved is based on the individual designer's experience with a particular market and/or customer and the core samples developed by the same designer. Each collection has a defined cost price range and the designers have to select materials and plan work content so that their samples fall within these limits. The core samples selected as the basis for each collection are those considered most suitable for a particular market or customer, and when appropriate the same core sample can be used more than once.

| | | | | | | |
|---|---|---|---|---|---|---|
| \multicolumn{7}{c}{SKIRT DESIGN PROGRAMME} |

| | SKIRT DESIGN PROGRAMME | | | | | |
|---|---|---|---|---|---|---|
| Season: Winter | | Phase: I | | Completion: 20/6 | | |

| Designer | Market / Customer | Cost Price range | Core samples | | | | Total |
|---|---|---|---|---|---|---|---|
| Jackie | Home | £18-£20 | 404 | 4106 | 4107 | / | 16 |
| Anne | Home | £22-£25 | 4111 | 4116 | 4118 | 4120 | 15 |
| Anne | Home / D+B | £18-£20 | 4121 | 4124 | 4127 | / | 12 |
| Jackie | Home / Adnac | £20-£22 | 4103 | 4108 | 4112 | 4122 | 12 |
| Janet | Export / U.S.A | $35-$40 | 4103 | 4104 | 4411 | 4118 | 12 |
| Janet | Export / Germany | DM45-DM50 | 404 | 4111 | 4126 | 4136 | 15 |
| | | | | | | | |
| | | | | | | Total: | 82 |

**Fig. 12.1.** Design programme.

## PRODUCTION PLANNING

Figure 12.2 shows an example of a production planning and control system. The principles of its operation are as follows.

It sets out in detail the planned deliveries of the sample room to the marketing department during one working week. The week itself is denoted by the international week numbering system and the matching dates. In this example, sample garments take four to five days (throughput time) to produce; some of the planned deliveries were commenced during the previous week and will be completed in the current week. The progress of each garment is controlled by entering the date when a key operation of its production is completed. These dates are obtained from the daily work sheets (see Fig. 12.3) completed by operators or supervisors. The lower part of Fig. 12.2 shows a summary of the daily and cumulative results. This system provides management with detailed and up to date information regarding sample production.

## REPORTING

The example of a daily work sheet shown in Fig. 12.3 is that for a sample cutter who records details of the garments cut and such additional information as is required. Other operators also use similar types of

| | | | SAMPLE PRODUCTION PLAN | | | | |
|---|---|---|---|---|---|---|---|

| Week Nº | Date | Planned deliveries | Jackets | Coats | Total |
|---|---|---|---|---|---|
| 18 | ¹⁶/₄ – ²⁰/₄ | | 20 | 15 | 35 |

| Style Nº | Garment | Cut | Sewn | Pressed | Inspected | Approved | Delivered |
|---|---|---|---|---|---|---|---|
| 6164 | Jkt. | 11/4 | 12/4 | 13/4 | 13/4 | 13/4 | 16/4 |
| 6166 | —..— | 10/4 | 11/4 | 12/4 | 13/4 | 13/4 | 16/4 |
| S404 | Coat | 10/4 | 11/4 | 12/4 | 13/4 | 13/4 | 16/4 |
| S405 | —..— | 10/4 | 11/4 | 12/4 | 13/4 | 16/4 | 16/4 |
| S406 | —..— | 11/4 | 12/4 | 13/4 | 16/4 | 16/4 | 16/4 |
| 6167 | Jacket | 11/4 | 12/4 | 13/4 | 16/4 | 16/4 | 17/4 |
| 6169 | —..— | 11/4 | 12/4 | 13/4 | 16/4 | 16/4 | 17/4 |
| S408 | Coat | 11/4 | 12/4 | 13/4 | 16/4 | 16/4 | 17/4 |
| S410 | —..— | 11/4 | 12/4 | 13/4 | 16/4 | 17/4 | 17/4 |
| 6168 | Jkt. | 12/4 | 13/4 | 16/4 | 17/4 | 17/4 | 17/4 |
| S411 | Coat | 12/4 | 13/4 | 16/4 | 17/4 | 17/4 | 17/4 |
| 6170 | Jkt | 12/4 | 13/4 | 16/4 | | | |

DAILY AND WEEKLY SUMMARY

| Date: | 16/4 | | 17/4 | | 18/4 | | 19/4 | | 20/4 | |
|---|---|---|---|---|---|---|---|---|---|---|
| Garment: | Jkts. | Coats | Jkts. | Coats | Jkts. | Coats | Jkts. | Coats | Jkts. | Coats |
| Delivery: | 3 | 3 | 4 | 3 | 4 | 4 | 5 | 3 | 4 | 4 |
| To date: | 3 | 3 | 7 | 6 | 11 | 10 | 16 | 13 | 20 | 17 |

**Fig. 12.2.** Production planning and control system.

| DAILY WORK SHEET | | | Date: 23/.4 | | |
|---|---|---|---|---|---|
| Name: Alisa | | Number: 2208 | | Job: Cutter | |

| Style number | Garment | Quantities | | | |
|---|---|---|---|---|---|
| | | Top cloth | Direction | Lining | Fusible |
| 6184 | Skirt | 0.70 | ⟶ | 0.65 | Band |
| 6185 | —..— | 0.75 | ⇄ | ╱ | —.— |
| 6186 | —..— | 0.70 | ⇄ | 0.65 | —.— |
| 4534 | Trousers | 1.15 | ⟶ | 0.75 | Band + 10cm |
| 4536 | —..— | 1.10 | ⇄ | ╱ | —..— |
| 4537 | —.— | 1.10 | ⟶ | ╱ | —..— |
| | | | | | |
| | | | | | |
| | | | | | |

| Jackets: ╱ | Skirts: 3 | Trousers: 3 | Total: 6 |
|---|---|---|---|

**Fig. 12.3.** Example of daily work sheet.

forms and all of these are used to control the progress of each garment during its production in the sample room.

## CONTROL SYSTEMS

Whatever reporting method is used, the most important factor is the practical relevance of the information conveyed by the report. The real bottom line for the manager is not how many buttonholes were sewn yesterday but the number of sample garments delivered to the marketing department the previous day. In addition, the manager also requires information regarding the exact status of all the samples planned to be produced during a specific period. This information is essential because if the manager sees or anticipates possible bottle-necks, remedial action can be taken before major problems occur.

A reporting system has to be selective regarding the type and extent of information it reports. Too much irrelevant information wastes people's time, and too little of the key information is inconclusive. So for a report to be effective, it has to be short and to the point. Conventional reporting systems work on a daily basis and the accumulated information can be summarised for or by the manager and also posted on a prominently displayed wall chart for all members of the staff to see.

## TO SUM UP

The management of a design department requires a large element of technocracy but as this department becomes larger, the quality of a manager is based less on technocratic ability and more on the manager as a person. Management is concerned with managing people and not with matching the colours of buttons. A manager lacking industrial social skills will at best only be capable of performing some, but not all, of the basic functions of good management.

# References

Carr, H. & Latham, B. (1994) *The Technology of Clothing Manufacture*, Second Edition. Blackwell Science, Oxford.

Friend, R.L. (1977) *Sewing Room Technical Handbook*, HATRA. The Research Centre for Knitting, Dyeing and Making-up, Nottingham.

Hudson, P.B. (1989) *Guide to Apparel Manufacturing*. Media Inc., Greensboro, North Carolina.

Solinger, J. (1988) *Apparel Manufacturing Handbook* (2nd edn). Bobbin Blenheim, Columbia, South Carolina.

## FURTHER READING

Carr, H. & Pomeroy, J. (1992) *Fashion Design and Product Development*. Blackwell Science, Oxford.

Cooklin, G. (1989) *Fusing Technology*. The Textile Institute, Manchester.

Cooklin, G. (1996) *Introduction to Clothing Manufacture* (2nd edn). Blackwell Science, Oxford.

Cooper, G.R. (1985) *The Sewing Machine – Its Invention and Development* (2nd edn). Smithsonian Press, Washington.

Hall, A.J. (1965) *The Standard Handbook of Textiles* (5th edn). Temple Press Books, London.

Lowe, J. & Lowcock, P.D. (1986) *An Approach to Quality Control in the Clothing Industry*. Emraine Publications, Ware, Herts.

Lyle, O. (1960) *The Efficient Use of Steam*. HMSO, London.

Trautman, J.E. (1979) *Materials Utilisation in the Apparel Industry*. Apparel Research Foundation, Arlington.

## COMPANY PUBLICATIONS

*How to Lay Checks*. Bullmerwerk GmbH, Mehrstetten, Germany.

*The Technology of Thread and Seams*. Coats Ltd, Enderby, Leicester.

*Fusing Without Risk*. Kannegiesser GmbH, Vlotho, Germany.

# *Index*